First Place, 2014 LuckyCinda Av
Winner, 2015 Beverly Hills Book
Finalist, 2018 International Book Awards in General Self Help
Distinguished Favorite, 2018 Independent Press Award in General Self Help
First Place, 2017-2018 Literary Award in Self-Help

"A perceptive, persuasive analysis of self-imposed suffering with a practical formula for relief and release … The set up is entertaining … the discussion is neither dry nor cut off from the heart …"
—KIRKUS REVIEWS

"Hartman speaks directly to the reader and often seems to be there in the room with you. He explains so much about how the mind can be affected by the pain and yearning of the past, and presents a means by which one can escape that hold and live more fully in the present. I was profoundly impacted by what I read within this book."
—Five Star review by Jack Magnus for READERS' FAVORITE

"With much wisdom and knowledge to be considered on the power of thought and finding that last bit we need to beat our fear, The Breakthrough is a strongly recommended addition to self-help and inspirational collections, highly recommended."
—THE MIDWEST BOOK REVIEW

"Dr. Hartman has created a self-help book unlike any other...the book is both a refreshing read and a surprisingly helpful guide to understanding how and why we experience anxiety, depression, and panic about our emotional states. By advocating an understanding and appreciation of our actual relationship to the universe (as opposed to a fanciful or childish holdover) we can begin to fully inhabit each moment of our lives. Using experimental font sizes, inventive dialogue in the format of a play, and carefully chosen anecdotes from his own life and experience, Hartman creates a memorable and helpful guide to reclaiming happiness and leaving behind nameless dread."
—IndieReader

"... amazingly smooth to read ... wonderful scene titles and quotes ... As complex as psychology is, the author has made it quite approachable to countless people - I would almost hope that this text becomes required reading for all teaching, nursing, political science, business, (in fact every subject) students, if not all high school students!"
—Five Star review by Melinda Hills for READERS' FAVORITE

"The Breakthrough in Two Acts, a remarkable evaluation, assessment, and practical revelation of human consciousness and our intimate connection with it, reads more like Fredric C. Hartman is a poet, not a doctor ... That is the pleasure one feels while reading: not like he is listening to a lecture, but like he has wandered into a private conversation revealing the big secret behind our existence ... the effect of Dr. Hartman's book is to make one feel enlightened, and yes, a bit more light-hearted. But, in a most down-to-earth and useful way ... Everyone needs to read this book. Everyone should read this book."
—Five Star review by Joel Dennstedt for READERS' FAVORITE

"The Breakthrough in Two Acts written by clinical psychologist Fredric C. Hartman is a transformative piece of non-fiction ... The tone is intelligent, but also so relatable that I feel even a pre-teen reader would be able to grasp parts of it. It's definitely a book that would have interested me at a young age ... I can easily say that The Breakthrough in Two Acts is an epiphany in written form ... You need this book, and your sister, brother, cousin, father, and mother. The stranger you don't know on the corner needs it. It'll change you and give comfort in a way that you never would have thought possible."
—Five Star review by Nicole Cochran for READERS' FAVORITE

THE BREAKTHROUGH
IN TWO ACTS

The Breakthrough in Two Acts
Breaking the Spells of Painful Emotions and Finding the Calm
in the Present Moment

iUniverse books may be ordered through booksellers or by contacting:

iUniverse
1663 Liberty Drive
Bloomington, IN 47403
www.iuniverse.com
1-800-Authors (1-800-288-4677)

Because of the dynamic nature of the Internet, any Web addresses or links contained in this book may have changed since publication and may no longer be valid.

ISBN: 978-1-5320-0926-6 (sc)
ISBN: 978-1-5320-0927-3 (hc)
ISBN: 978-1-5320-0928-0 (e)

Library of Congress Control Number: 2016917867

Print information available on the last page.

iUniverse Rev. 01/28/2020

Publisher's Cataloging-in-Publication data

Names: Hartman, Fredric C., author.
Title: Breakthrough in two acts : breaking the spells of painful emotions
and finding the calm in the present moment / Fredric C. Hartman, Ph.D.
Description: Bloomington, IN: iUniverse, 2017.
Identifiers: ISBN 978-1-5320-0926-6.
Subjects: LCSH Self-actualization (Psychology) | Self psychology. |
Consciousness. | Meditation. | BISAC PSYCHOLOGY / Emotions
Classification: LCC BF637.M4 .H37 2017 | DDC 158.1/2--dc23

For everyone I've worked with
and everyone I haven't

To Amanda and Julie

And to Celia

And K

All that a man has to say or do that can possibly concern mankind, is in some shape or other to tell the story of his love,—to sing…

Henry David Thoreau
Journal, 6 May 1854

Nothing is at last sacred but the integrity of our own mind … Nothing can bring you peace but yourself.

Ralph Waldo Emerson
Self-Reliance (1832)

Contents

Act II Breaking Free of Painful Emotions and Being in the Present Moment, and I Mean Being in the Present Moment

Two Obstacles to Believing in the Possibility of Changing Ourselves

Here are Seven Routes You Could Take Out of the Pain in Your Past and into the Serenity in This Moment. They Were Found by a Search Party of Thousands Scouring the Higher and Lower Elevations in My Office.

The Urgent Reason for Referral

Cassius:

> *"The fault, dear Brutus, is not in our stars,*
> *But in ourselves, that we are underlings."*

William Shakespeare
Julius Caesar (1599)

Long ago, during moments of the most luminous insight, humans conceived of harvesting grain and proceeded to nourish themselves in a new way. They settled down in one place to farm, establishing an enduring sense of home. Their numbers grew and civilization was born. They had achieved a freedom from danger unknown to any other animal on the Earth. Consciousness was set free to play, to wonder and to see more deeply into the character of things in the world and the skies above. Ingenious devices and discoveries were made. Culture emerged that spread wealth, knowledge and joy. And, to this day, humanity keeps inventing new ways of gaining mastery over danger.

But before this new era, the species roamed the planet. It had to hunt and gather its food, move with the herds, the seasons, and keep a sharp and wary focus on survival, each member so vulnerable to predators and other dangers and cooperating in a tight hierarchy. Their number were kept low by this. What helped them cope with this uneasy way of life was a network of fast nerves that evolved deep inside their brain which would be acutely aware of the ever-present danger around them. This web of nerves protected them, as it does all the other animals living in the wild, by sending up surges of dark emotion as alarm signals, which mirror looming danger, so they could strike with their weapons forcefully enough, and survive. This nerve web grew to be so powerful because it collected in its cells an enormous number of old memories of scenes that led to death.

Even though humans were much safer once their habitat shifted from the wilderness to settled civilization, this protective nerve web in their brains, by its neurological design, still went on believing danger was everywhere. And because it has had the power to reign so decidedly over consciousness, instead of the other way around, its dominion in the new habitat of civilization has gone largely unchecked throughout history. It goes on aiming its self-preserving aggression now at fellow humans on all different scales and causes havoc everywhere.

Consciousness continues to undergo its great expansion, like the whole universe, its calm wonderment reaching in every direction, fashioning dazzling tools and improving its joy and safety. Many do realize they are safer and more fortunate so much more of the time than that wary, primitive network in their brain believes they are. What they don't realize yet is how destructive, how lethal, this very network in their brain can be. If they did, they would target it head-on with their own more discerning view of the actual degree of danger out there, and quiet it down at last. It would be a grand moment of truth and mark the dramatic changing of a paradigm in the species.

But until this happens, feelings of darkness and foreboding will keep spreading through the world, echoing often in the news and permeating civilization with its harsh responses and grim consequences—with emotional illness, corruption and crime, oppression, genocide and war.

The ready conviction in the species of believing danger is everywhere has steadily intensified as numbers have grown along with advancing technology and has reached a very critical moment. There is a sign looming that this species is now clearly suffering from a major depression and has gone into crisis, despite its lighter moments. Not long ago it discovered a sure method—atomic and hydrogen bombs—which could achieve its annihilation in the length of an afternoon. And as a species with thoughts of suicide, it flirts now and then with visions of the end. Humanity has entered a dangerous, fateful time in its relationship with itself.

This is why Human Consciousness has to be referred for intensive psychotherapy.

The Characters

Dr. Hartman, a psychologist
Human Consciousness

The Setting

On the far right of the stage, a door opens into a small waiting room carpeted in green, with two upholstered wooden chairs and an end table between them on which a lamp glows softly. A coat stand and a magazine rack are on either side of the entrance door. Hanging on the wall is a painting of a still life.

A short way across the stage from the right is the door to Dr. Hartman's office. Inside, his office looks like a living room. The back and left walls of this corner office are all windows, giving a panoramic view of the town in the full bloom of springtime. Against the back wall of windows is a brown couch. On the left is Dr. Hartman's brown, swiveling easy chair and on the right is a bentwood, free-form chair in green leather.

The Beginning

The lights go down to total darkness and come back up.

Old music is playing in the waiting room.

Human Consciousness is sitting in the chair furthest from the door to Dr. Hartman's office, trying to read a magazine. Dr. Hartman is in his office on his way to the waiting room door.

DR. HARTMAN: Emerges into the waiting room and looks across at Human Consciousness with a hint of a smile. "Hello," he says, "Come in."

HUMAN CONSCIOUSNESS: Puts the magazine in the rack and follows Hartman into the office, becoming a little tentative, trying to take it all in.

DR. HARTMAN: "Anywhere you like." As he sits in his chair.

HUMAN CONSCIOUSNESS: Looks around a little more at the furnishings and sits down in the free-form bentwood chair opposite Hartman's, bouncing a little in it, looking at Hartman and feeling a little odd.

Overture to Just One:

Consciousness, You Mean the World to Me

[*Hartman is sitting in his chair, crossing a leg. Among other things in this scene, Human Consciousness is drawn to the sounds of trucks and cars driving by, and a jet flying overhead, and a bee that keeps bumping into the window behind Hartman. No matter how many people may be present in the theater of life and no matter what Hartman tries to say or how fervently he says it, sometimes it seems that Human Consciousness is barely listening, barely there.*]

Let's stop kidding ourselves. Whenever anyone comes to me for help, it's the awareness that enters my office which needs the help. It's not a man and it's not a woman. My real patient is human awareness, which is not something we just have; it's what we *are*; it's *all* we are. It's this one single awareness I seize hold of the best I can. And I try to work a change into it. And now on this stage I finally get my hands on the whole troubled, gifted human thing.

And no, this is not a book or a play, exactly. And it's not a vaudeville variety show, either. It's an appeal, a very urgent appeal directly to awareness, my own included, to learn to see a different way, to dare to undertake the task of breaking free from the grip of the old emotions in our brain that can pull us into such dire views of the present moment. It's a holler, a shout. It's a yell, a yell full of love, the kind of yell a psychologist utters. Because you, Consciousness, can be some of the trickiest material to handle that this wide world has ever known. What it really takes to do this job thoroughly is a good, solid, evolved culture. But until our culture is equal to the task, lone practitioners like me will take it on. I'll try, in this room, to rival the power of a culture. I'll try to do what it can't do yet. I'll be everything you need me to be to help make you strong and healthy.

I'll be your obstetrician and deliver you right into this moment. And all that screaming in my delivery room will help, too. There'll be crying, and new life will begin.

And I'll be your pediatrician. I'll immunize you, take care of your illnesses and watch you grow. I'll be your dentist. And it might feel like pulling teeth sometimes or maybe like a root canal. I'll fill cavities, do cleanings and make bridges if necessary.

I'll be your teacher and teach you a lesson or two about life.

Or I'll be your auto mechanic. I'll help fix your flat or fill your radiator, fix your transmission, replace your battery. I'll do a tune-up or install a set of brakes. I'll also be your highway patrol officer and pull you over for driving too fast, recklessly, for not using a seatbelt, being drunk! And I'll be your judge and jury and find you guilty. I'll also find you very innocent.

And I'll be your cardiologist and take care of your broken heart. I'll do open heart surgery if I have to.

Usually anyone in your seat would do most of the talking in therapy. Well, not this time. I'll be your entertainer, your song and dance man, and try to make you smile. I'll sing out this big love song to win your heart. And I'll take you to the rodeo and be the announcer of your show as you find out what it means to ride that bucking limbic system of yours. I'll be your stand-up comic and try to make you laugh with the truth. Because there's a lot of show biz in this business of psychotherapy, my friend. It's a serious performance. It's high theater, because the stakes are so high.

So I'll sell you a ticket and take it at the door. I'll give you a program and show you to your seat. I'll be the announcer before every scene, give the stage directions and be a stagehand to work the lights and the curtain. I'll create that exciting moment full of anticipation before the show begins, and that silent, fateful moment after it ends.

And through it all I'll be your philosopher, getting at the truth in you, getting to the bottom of things. I'll be your artist and your poet and try to help you see what's so very beautiful inside. I'll even be your lepidopterist and help turn you into a butterfly.

I'll be your priest, your rabbi, or your minister and lift your spirit high. I'll pray to God for you, to any god I can find: the god of putting things into words, the god of insight, the god of pausing before you haul off, the god of responsibility, the god of fun and the god of love.

I'll go to extremes and try anything to help you not get pulled back into the old pain in your past, where you get lost and completely vanish from the here and now, as the pain takes you over and does the speaking for you. I'll be anything and everything for you, Consciousness, to help set you free to be in this moment. I will. Because, Consciousness ... I love you. I really do. You've travelled so very far already. And you're all we humans have to handle this universe. Do you hear me? Consciousness? Hello!?

Lights down to darkness.

Overture to the Whole World of Humans:

Is There Anyone in the House Who Wants an Emotional Breakthrough?
And Oh that Civilization! When Will it Want One?

Lights come up.

[Hartman swivels his chair around to face the audience. Human Consciousness is offstage thinking what a mess it is to have to be here and that this show must go on. From here on Human Consciousness will be referred to simply as Consciousness. Simply]

And now a brief word about humanity:

We live our lives assuming our minds are perfectly sound and everything is quite okay with us. We dress ourselves. We open and close doors commandingly and with poise. We speak with other people without any strain or pain. We make purchases with a sense of ease. We sail along in our cars smoothly.

Until there's an obstacle: a door that won't open, a difficult person, a broken dream.

But even then we're thankful that Time carries us on to help us cope. We get busy and distracted from whatever distressing emotion may flare up without much thought that they flare all too often for us humans and must be taking some kind of toll. But we forget and our sense that all is well gets restored once more.

And so we live, implicitly putting tremendous faith in Time to carry us as though it were a god. And we count on the blessed ride of Time, and forgetfulness, to save us from realizing with any urgency that it might be a good idea to do something else about this pain. As long as there's no obstacle large or persistent enough to set off one of those disabling storms called panic or depression, we tend to feel little need to do anything at all about the moment-to-moment condition of our minds. We assume, as we go along, that there will be no heavy weight to lift up with our minds, rather than building strength into them in the event circumstances develop that make it necessary to do that lifting. And circumstances will surely develop at some point that will make it necessary. But what we usually do instead is depend heavily on the luck of the draw, gambling all of our chips that the next moment we're carried to will be easier on us.

So who are we fooling? Civilization goes on condoning this way of living, and has for thousands and thousands of years. Yet I notice, too—and it seems almost like a well-kept secret—that so very many people are aware of the ocean of psychological pain in the world of humans: all of the disconnect and miscommunication, all of the destructiveness and anguish. The large mind of civilization has yet to instill in our hearts that it is urgently important to change all of this. But shouldn't a sturdy, stable awareness be as basic to civilized life as our physical health or having a safe home?

Lights go down.

Prologue

My Own Search for that All-Powerful Pause Called Serenity

*A man travels the world in search of what he needs
and returns home to find it.*

George Moore,
Anglo-Irish novelist
The Brook Kerith (1916)

Lights come up.

[*Hartman swivels around to face Consciousness, now back on stage. Among
other things in this scene, Consciousness thinks about Hartman's own weaknesses and struggles, and the ironies in his life—working up a kind of diagnosis
of him.*]

For so long, so very long, I opposed and avoided psychology. I despised it.
It seemed like a load of mumbo jumbo. All this about "parts" of the mind:
id, ego, and superego. A personal unconscious and a collective unconscious.
A real self and a false self. Blah, blah, blah. Like seeing things in clouds and
believing they're actually up there.

But in spite of this, for as long as I can remember, I've been on a definite
search for some kind of inner peace, a hunt for some kind of serenity. Not
the way weekend turkey hunters hunt, but the way a hungry animal hunts:
going here and there, picking up scents, and not thinking much. And I

wasn't hunting just for that feeling of serenity you get from kicking back and relaxing; I wanted to feel it in the very thick of things, when my mind was being thrown off by life, as it seemed so often to be. I probably wouldn't have been able to admit to my search if I was asked about it. I was unaware of myself and quite inarticulate. Reading was a supreme strain for me. I didn't like to read much until after college.

So for most of my formative years, I did have a strong inner sense about things, but one that was deep in an anxious haze and impossible to spell out to myself except in a blunt, mute sort of way. This made my psychological life a very tricky business. Life was a comedy and tragedy of trial and error. I felt like a creature roaming and stumbling through a forest.

I watched a lot of TV in the late 1950s, the '60s and '70s. I believed so much in the characters portrayed in those shows that I thought I could get real clues about finding my own serenity. I took guitar lessons after I heard The Beatles, hoping I could make music that was as serene and moving as theirs. Some of their melodies steadied me into such an inspired calm, holding me there for so long after the songs ended. I played baseball, believing the gracefulness of the plays held the secret of that poised, calm feeling I was searching for. The crack of the bat and the way it felt catching a fly ball were so fine I wanted to spend the rest of my life playing baseball so the feeling would come again and again. In all of this, I knew I wasn't just living my life, being a child, having fun, or learning skills. I was definitely after something I couldn't tell myself I was after. I couldn't have cared less about my awareness. It was beside the point. I was chasing something I thought was out there in the world, not anywhere inside.

I also tried to prolong the moments when I was in a picturesque scene because serenity was right there: the hushed winter mornings when I would cocoon in my home under the deep blankets of snow covering my neighborhood; or the drowsy, lazy summer afternoons with the sound of cicadas everywhere, strangely amplifying the stillness of my street. I remember gazing at my tropical fish, wanting to capture the secret of their calm as they swam so smoothly through their lives. And there was that inexplicable feeling of wonderment that overcame me at the sight of a pretty girl. I wasn't just enjoying these experiences for how they moved me in the moment, although

I did that. I was searching, in my lost and unconscious way, for something I could graft onto myself permanently. But serenity was accidental and fleeting wherever I found it. I couldn't make it last.

I became drawn to subjects like hypnosis, especially self-hypnosis. The idea of positive thinking also intrigued me for a while. None of it worked for long.

So I was driven to more ecstatic experiences. I got drunk and high a number of times and romped around with friends. It was entertaining but didn't lead me to what I was after, either. I dated, fell madly in love, and was shattered. And something about this astounded me even while I was being tormented by it. Instead of love came the sharpest pain.

On to college. Reluctantly, I was persuaded to major in a new hybrid called psychobiology. I still had no use for psychology, still didn't think it had legitimacy as a branch of knowledge. The professor of my first course, Introduction to Psychology, also wrote the textbook. I was surprised how intelligible it was to me, considering how poorly read I was at that point in my life. But my deep skepticism for the field held fast. It still all seemed like it was made out of purely personal opinion—not a real science, like physics or chemistry.

Also, while at NYU, I was a premed student. Why? Because of a moment in 1958. I was four and had recently moved from an apartment in the Bronx to a house in Wantagh, Long Island. I remember that day so vividly. My relatives were visiting for some occasion. The cast of characters were all arrayed in the living room. It was one of those winter afternoons when dusty, nervous sunbeams were slanting in. I was asked what I wanted to be when I grew up. I remember not being able to hold back these words: "I want to be a people doctor." And such joy surged through that living room, such a gratified murmur spread through that audience by my idea of becoming a doctor, that I fell deeply under its spell. I began to daydream about becoming a physician, the only kind of doctor I knew of. There was a toy I couldn't wait to get: a clear human body with organs you could remove to identify and marvel at. Love and passion were in the air, and maybe a promise of enduring serenity. The winds of this spell swirled through my adolescence. I watched every TV medical drama there was. I felt like I was bound for some kind of priesthood. In college, the spell drove me into high gear, and I was determined to get in to medical school.

When I finally got there, the disappointment was as crushing as my first breakup. Although the science was familiar and manageable, it dawned on me almost immediately that the serenity I was searching for would not be found there, either. The spell I was under for all those years broke completely and I awoke from it feeling dreadfully lost. I did enjoy working on my cadaver, though. I enjoyed it immensely. He was a shoemaker who died from an aortic aneurism, probably almost instantly and peacefully. We were exhorted by our anatomy professor to regard our cadavers with the utmost reverence as we took them apart from foot to brain. Seeing what was in this human body and how it was designed gave me the only hints of awe and serenity I had there. Otherwise, medical school was just another false lead.

So I left after one year and returned to New York City with a primitive inkling that the trail was back there somewhere. Another romantic relationship started and ended. My ex-girlfriend suggested I get help from a psychotherapist. Here was psychology again. I was still skeptical, but the pain and confusion were terrific now.

I went to a clinic in Manhattan, where a therapist was assigned to me. He was a balding, lanky, quiet man. I couldn't imagine how this guy could ever help me get out of my pain, let alone help me find serenity. I started to speak and then stopped. I made a few more false starts then stopped for weeks. Silence. Frozen on the couch with this stranger sitting there behind me, relaxed, waiting.

When I finally began to speak again, the discussions were about trying to clarify what I was expecting of myself, of humanity, of life. I was a very hard sell. Bernie, my therapist, bore the brunt of my skepticism about psychology. But he wasn't particularly thrown or deterred. He kept talking (when he talked) about this thing in my mind, this "should" banging away inside and wearying me of the world. He kept on describing it, as though it were a constellation in the sky. He continued pointing it out until I actually began to see a pattern. Something was happening to me. But it took time. I began to realize, in the throes of a huge feeling of letdown, that all of the serenity I dreamed of could be mine only if I was able to do the impossible and control the uncontrollable.

Sad but liberating realizations came. The way I wished for serenity and the intensity, were the very problems. Bernie led me to see a powerful source of energy inside, but one that was haywire, fooling me, stressing me. Serenity was a good thing in principle, but I had to face the reason for my urgent need for it—old thought patterns left over from my childhood which drove me so hard. I had to give up hoping my happiness should come from the outside world and let the world off the hook. It was important to learn to see my inner world the way an astronomer studies the skies: appreciating a whole universe in my mind inhabited by mysteries and moving with great forces. I had to keep making a strong, unnatural effort to see the way old thinking gets stirred up inside me, with its yearnings for magic or possibly more pained demands for it, and to see it all from the perspective of this very moment. It was my only real hope. And I realized that, like all incompletely evolved creatures, I would need to keep exploring it and working on it until my very last moment, and that it was okay to never be finished, and to have setbacks.

Once, my mind felt nearly nonexistent to me. I didn't look there for much, even though I—my entire awareness—was inside of it all the time and it was actually the only place where I could ever be or go. I was deeply skeptical of psychology. All those models of the mind seemed clunky to me, like something you would make with an Erector Set. And I struggled with that painful aversion to reading when I was a child that was as strong as my love is for it now. There's still a definite lack of sophistication to the quality of my experience, whether I read or not. And I can still be pulled back into old negative feeling and succumb to the old painful wishing. But my mind and my awareness are much more special to me now, despite all of my quirks and limitations. More special, maybe, because I realize now more deeply than ever that they're all I will ever have to work with. There's no place like home.

Lights down.

In order to arrive at what you are not
You must go through the way in which you are not.

T. S. Eliot
Four Quartets (1943)

… enter the language of transformation!

Mary Oliver
Thirst (2006)

Introduction

The Written Word, the Spoken Word, and the Word that Changes You Forever and a Day

There is a road, no simple highway
Between the dawn and the dark of night

The Grateful Dead
Ripple (1970)

Lights come up.

[Hartman, in a cone of warm yellow light, swivels around to face the audience. Consciousness is restless in the shadow.]

This is a story about time, and the time travel that goes on inside our brain. It's the story about the way Human Consciousness lives its life, the way it falls through the time inside our minds back into the past, helplessly, and sometimes dangerously. And it's about the way it undertakes the heroic journey back again into this present moment, where it does its greatest work and can experience its most profound wisdom and peace.

I've dreamed of creating a kind of experience which might help bring a reader, an audience, to see what's at the flash point of a major personal transformation. And I don't mean just a feeling of hope or inspiration. I want for people to see what I've seen inside the mind, what astounding things it's made of: how the primitive past lives right there inside our brain, and how to decipher and break the hypnotic spell we call emotional pain, which comes from that past. I also want to convey some things I've learned

1

about the nature of the present moment, and how I believe we can mobilize our strength in order to feel steady, serene, resilient, and newly alive to it. And by doing this, I wanted to create something that might shorten how long it would take to have a life-changing breakthrough.

*   *   *

Books which teach us humans how to live have been written for almost as long as we've had the written word. Each of these books of self-improvement has a narrator speaking in a voice that's positive and confident. It's as though this voice is coming from a person who has already undergone a major breakthrough, has made peace with the hardships of life, and now has considerable strength of mind to accept life's limitations and fully appreciate its blessings and wonders.

In many books, the voice of the narrator is glowing with positive feeling and encouragement, explaining and asking questions along the way, and perhaps providing exercises that steer the reader toward change. In another kind of self-improvement book is a voice, radiant with a spiritual faith, which speaks of humanity as destined for a golden age when all will possess greater powers of enlightenment and love if we can start now to embrace certain new values and ways of being.

The prose in these books is often studded with tightly compressed truths and reassuring directives about what to change and how, and what the outcome of the effort will be: "You can believe in yourself." "Quiet your mind." "Practice humility." "Know that you can do it." "Live in the moment." "Love yourself."

The uplift from a self-help book can feel like alchemy. Mastery of life's woes seems at hand. These books leave very warm, powerful spells in their wakes that temporarily break the one that is our pain and inspire us to believe that the pain can be gone for good.

But I see two big problems with them. The first is an overemphasis on the positive. All of my work as a psychologist has shown me that positive thinking alone is not enough to achieve deep, lasting change until the grip of negative thinking, which can be far more powerful, is broken. The second problem is that truths about how to live, however comforting or inspiring, don't help a person contend with the very strains of the journey, with what has to go on in a person's awareness during those very moments of transformation when change is actually happening.

So although these books can cast fabulous spells, the spells are short-lived. They don't quite reach all the way to the heart of the problem or the solution and so don't alter the course of anyone's life in a lasting way. What does develop between a reader and the uplifting prose in self-improvement books is a very inspiring resonance which gets mistaken for that strengthened state of mind not yet possible to produce without the help of the book. So hope surges up high for a while on the book's energy, and then slowly subsides, leaving readers in the same state of potential they were in before they read it.

I've wanted to tell the amazing story, distilled from the work I've done all these years, about what happens to our awareness when negative emotions flare up from a feral old place deep inside our brain, and how, when it's not strong, our awareness falls quickly and helplessly under the anguishing hypnotic spells of these emotions, and then what goes on—what thinking we need to do—to break these spells and move back freely into the vast, fleeting, present moment of life again. I want to help create a change in someone with the dramatic words I use in this performance the way I do in my office with the ones I speak there.

*　　　　*　　　　*

Out there in civilization, there's a certain disturbing threshold, which this book, this show, aims to lower. It's a threshold of concern about emotional pain and havoc in life, below which emotional pain is barely noticed and gets disregarded altogether, and above which it is devastating and extremely urgent to do something about immediately. What's so disturbing to me about this threshold is that by the time it's reached, there's so much pain, so much mess to repair: government corruption hitting the news, a huge Ponzi scheme, a sexual abuse scandal, a shooting spree that erupts suddenly after so many ominous signs were ignored, a genocide underway with so many lives already lost and so many watching in silence. And this threshold in civilization has barely moved for thousands of years.

So what I see from the chair in my office is that there's all of this subtle pain just about everywhere, in all of us. It's in awareness and below awareness, flaring, subsiding, and flaring again so much of the time. I can see it everywhere I go: in grocery stores and companies; in the media; in neighbors, friends, and relatives, and in myself. Low-grade emotional pain is rising and falling throughout the day, throughout the seasons of our lives. But it's far below that threshold of concern in our culture's mind which we've taken our lead from for so long. So it all gets neglected until it grows and grows, as it almost always does sooner or later.

But even this smaller, subtler pain means that something is wrong with the way we're thinking about things. It means there's something wrong with our awareness that it weakens so under the strain of too much negative emotion. It would become a much healthier world if concern about ordinary emotional pain could be triggered sooner so we could figure out a way to handle it better.

There's never been any society-wide teaching about this, or about that strangest of realms called the mind, in a way that could be decisively useful or practical to all of us. Nor has there been any formal teaching about this all-encompassing thing we're all living in right now called the present moment. Civilization as a whole isn't particularly interested in these two things. But what else is there but our minds and our experience of this very moment?

And serenity? What about serenity—feeling centered and calm? Our culture, it seems, couldn't care much less about it.

So let's make this clear to ourselves: our culture doesn't appear to be passionately concerned about emotional pain, awareness, the mind in general, with the nature of this moment we're always in, or with helping to generate for its citizens some kind of moment-to-moment serenity in life.

And so when we're faced with a serious jolt to our circumstances and a large wave of turmoil hits us, all we know how to do is flail around and reach in vain for the comforts, distractions, or quick fixes we're used to reaching for. Or we pray for that blessed movement of time to carry us along into the next moment which, we hope, will take us far away from the pain.

But at some point, there will likely come a crisis, a calamity, a catastrophe, that will make us shudder. And we won't know how to handle it well or at all, because we don't know how to handle all of those much smaller waves of pain that rise up into so many of our passing moments—the little waves like feelings of exasperation, anxiety, etc., (a thorough list is waiting for you in scene 9).

It may be true that a serious crisis can be great for bringing about deep change in a person. I've seen it happen often in my work. Tragedies have a remarkable power to set off and accelerate great personal transformations. Because if to change means to have a richer relationship with the present moment of your life, then a tragedy or trauma of some kind can certainly rivet your attention on the present moment like nothing else, changing your relationship with it forever. But what a way to bring about change! What havoc and blows to basic security and trust come with this kind of change.

But it's actually not the catastrophe that creates new strength. It's the interest, the motivation, and the urgency to find that strength which gets shocked into being and mobilized by the catastrophe.

Life shouldn't have to become such a painful mess in order for us to get a hold of ourselves and avert those messes and all the anguish that comes. But because of where that threshold of concern happens to be in the mind of our culture, we can get lulled into believing it's unnecessary to activate ourselves at all. Once it was hard to build shelters and bake bread, and to learn to read and do math. But it all happened with the right effort, and it has helped us all live better lives.

We can learn to build new strength into ourselves without all the subtle and not so subtle crashing and burning we do on a daily basis. It might seem a bit too much to ask of the words in these pages, the words coming from this stage, to do this. But in my office, time after time, I've helped shake awareness out of its slumber and into a wakefulness it hadn't thought possible. Maybe a good shaking can come from a performance like this book, too.

*   *   *

What you're about to experience is a single psychotherapy session with an entire treatment telescoped into it; it contains all of the ideas and perspectives necessary for the journey to the "cure." Along the way I cajole my "patient," I tease, I raise and quiet my voice, I send subliminal signals. In the name of truth, I play.

In Act I, I introduce the mind as I see it. I define what emotional pain is, and then I proceed to dissect a single negative emotion all the way to the heart of why and how it has its distorting, painful effect on our consciousness. In Act II, I focus on becoming free of emotional pain, and offer my take on the nature of the present moment and what I think it might mean to really be in it.

After 30 years, and a 100,000 sessions, I continue to be astounded by the process of doing psychotherapy. It has potential that has barely begun to be realized, like humankind's first use of fire or first attempts to fly. And I include in the term "therapy" all of the many different forms of psychotherapy, counseling, life coaching, and the healing of faith that have been developed to suit the whole spectrum of personality styles.

Therapy's very reason for being is to help create a change. Unlike other ways that help us change without any intervention, like accidents or traumas, therapy involves deliberately activating yourself in the gentlest and most methodical way. It means using the power and precision of language to *see* into your own brain, and to stir up the force of will to set off a transformation. A session costs what a good hairdo costs. And a whole course of therapy costs about as much as a trip to Europe or a car. But it doesn't cost nearly as much as the devastation that comes from being unprepared for emotional jolts, or from neglecting a mess in the making.

There are lots of misconceptions about therapy. Sometimes people believe that simply knowing what the problem is should be the goal and purpose of psychotherapy. But this isn't so. If the journey to the breakthrough point and a changed outlook on life is, say, a hundred miles, just *knowing* the problem may only take you about five. The rest of the journey is the *process* of the transformation, the redesigning and metamorphosis of awareness itself. The power of psychotherapy lies in its exact, moment-by-moment method for teaching our awareness how to have a breakthrough and free itself, maybe for the first time, from the grip of a deeper, ferocious old part of the brain, and then how to do it again and again, more and more easily, as the challenging circumstances of life call for.

Another misconception about therapy is that what does the work is a good relationship with a therapist. A good relationship is certainly important. It blends the ingredients of friendliness, candor, a basic love of life shared, and the collaboration to generate interest in the journey of learning how to use catalytic ideas for a transformation of yourself. A good therapist is, after all, a finely tuned human presence whose language works as a kind of instrument, a navigational device, to help show the way into your mind. There, with this skilled person, you can learn to see into the vastness and complexity inside, learn how it all works, and resonate with those turning-point ideas, as the remodeling of your awareness proceeds. A tuned, human presence is also helpful to respond to all of those questions that need to be asked to sharpen the focus, and all of the doubts and sorrows that need to be shared along the way. But it's the method itself planted in your mind during the course of psychotherapy which will be used to transform yourself long after the relationship with your therapist has ended.

And one of the worst misunderstandings about therapy is that it might threaten to somehow diminish a person's individuality or take away his or her uniqueness. But the contrary is true; therapy is there to throw light on our uniqueness, to empower it, so we can set it free from the spells of painful emotions and savor it more fully.

Undergoing an emotional breakthrough is an experience like finding a calling or raising a child. A personal transformation can be as much a great private work of art as any that has ever been created, and greater still because it is a creation vibrantly alive in us. And like other great works of art, its influence will reach far and wide into the world and future generations.

But I've always believed therapy doesn't need to take quite as long as it often does. When that first breakthrough occurs, it tends to happen quickly, in a matter of days or even moments. It's the preparation that takes time. It takes time to help someone commit to this unfamiliar, but most direct way of changing, to realize what and where the real problem is (inside your brain) and is not (the world). It takes time to learn how to focus the beams of your awareness inwardly as never before, how to handle the rumblings that accompany this kind of focus, and how to deal with the loss of old ways and learn to help the people in your life adapt well to the changes in you. So the process of psychotherapy can have some intricate, unexpected moments and passages, but at its best it's brain-changing and life-altering.

*   *   *

This show you're about to see is a kind of operation and repair manual, a complete course in what can go wrong with our minds (Act I) and how I believe it goes right (Act II). But more than this, it's my rendering of the story arc of a psychological breakthrough, as I've had a hand in it and have watched it go, from the careful seeding of ideas to their hidden growth and then, at the culmination of Act II, to a leap out into the unknown with strength to brave the struggle and confusion which proceed the most affirming moments of illumination.

Attempting to describe those points depicting the zone at which one large emotional paradigm shifts into a new one has felt like one of the best, most difficult things there is that I could do. I've used language as colorful, vivid and animated as I could find, and any difficulties grasping it or shortcomings you experience would clearly be all my doing.

There will be some neuroscience and quantum and astrophysics to see along the way, but only as colors on a canvas. This is a book of very sharp contrasts between the parts of our mind and between the inside of it and the outside, the deepest within and the farthest beyond. It's a study in how our awareness is made to see.

The higher purpose of it all is to craft and build a mindset that might open up a more direct way to wisdom, and use it as a vision and a force to help break beyond the confining paradigm that has been our familiar human way. And I've tried to link all of these parts in a sequence to make a smooth arc like in a song or a symphony. The effect of it all would be to turn more consistently positive, not so much with high-flying joy and exhilaration, but from a calm strength we steadily work into our thoughts to meet the living moments of life.

I can claim no ownership of the ideas I express here. I discovered them the way people find minerals in the ground. They're all old ideas I've rediscovered firsthand in my private practice. They've already been expressed in numerous ways by numberless people throughout human history. Beyond the native intelligence I possess, I know I have no great charisma to speak of, nor any extraordinary verbal gifts. But I do love human minds, and I love traveling them. And I'm blessed to have been invited for so many years by so many people into these private, most sacred of all places. Beyond all of the illusions, stigma, and glamour about psychotherapy, it is enigmatic, hallowed work to experience the sounds, images, and music in people's lives, and to spend my days working to help mobilize the potential in them.

Working on this book felt like I was preparing a gift. It contains what seems to me is the essence of the interaction—a kind of pheromone exchange—in a place called an office, that looks more like a living room, between someone who wants so much to give help and someone who wants so much to receive it. And most urgently of all, for these fateful times we're in, I wanted to offer a chant of ideas that could ignite some wonder. And from the wonder, inspiration. And from the inspiration, the will and commitment to break the hypnotic grip of threat and fear coming from the deep past inside our brain, plaguing our species so, and to move more comfortably into the teeming immensity of this present moment—the only actual moment we can ever have.

Lights down.

A Short Guide for the Moments to Come—
Can I Interest Anyone in Some Growing Pains?

Oh I can't, I can't get used to something so right …
Something so right.

Paul Simon
Something So Right (1973)

Lights come up.

[*Hartman swivels back to face Consciousness, but sometimes swivels around to face the audience. Among other things in this scene, Consciousness has an urge to quit therapy if it weren't for the reason for the referral, to just get up, walk out of the office and leave the building. Hartman notes the blank looks in Consciousness's eyes.*]

Why is it so hard to change? Throughout the ages we've heard about great illuminations, revelations, epiphanies, and awesome religious experiences that have changed people profoundly. And they're wonderful when they happen. But why so accidental? What about the idea of *working* on a breakthrough, the way a shoemaker works on making a shoe? You work on the shoe, and then, when you're done, you have a shoe. Why not the same with our minds when it comes to making a much needed change? Because the idea of *working* on our minds isn't so easy to apply to the vapor, the clouds and the air that seem to fill its atmosphere. How do you work on air?

But psychological change is actually a metamorphosis like any in nature. Like the frogs and the butterflies undergo. You—the psychological you—transform into something different, yet you remain, in essence, who you are. It's as though our minds are just like the patterns at the end of those old-fashioned kaleidoscopes with all the colored chips inside. There you are as a pattern, and when the barrel turns enough, you vanish then reappear as a completely different pattern. Same substance—different pattern. But when it comes to changing yourself, you're not only the pattern in the kaleidoscope, you're also the hand that turns the barrel. *You* make it happen and *you* feel what it's like to turn from one pattern into the other. You lose yourself and gain yourself, simultaneously.

When someone you know who's been in therapy has changed, or has changed as a result of some other kind of experience, it's very noticeable and looks dramatic and complete in its own way, yet there's no real sense of what might have gone on during the process. But on the inside of the person, while the change was actually happening (if it was a real and lasting change), there was more strenuous activity than the calm and poised outcome would lead you to believe.

During this play, I'm not after a surging, self-help-book kind of high, but a measure of real, quiet change. So it would be best to experience it slowly, only a few scenes at a time. In Act I, I want to take your awareness to that strange source of threatened and threatening emotions which exists inside every person's brain. To begin with, it won't be so easy to see what's there. There's no getting around this. It has to do with a part of the very problem—the human tendency to prefer looking outward and beyond in a rush, instead of within slowly. You'll have to accustom yourself to working in a new way inside this mysterious yet familiar old place.

And you'll need to have realizations, and big ones, to get this work done. And they'll cause a kind of growing pain. Some realizations will occur from experiencing this performance. But a lot of others, and maybe the most powerful, catalytic ones, will happen without words, during very private acts of synthesis. Maybe while you're driving, or at work, or in the shower, or falling asleep or waking up.

Early in this work, it'll seem like nothing much is happening at all. The pattern at the other end of the kaleidoscope will seem to be holding still. But there will be a strange little tension in it. And you want this tension to build. The new pattern, the one you don't see yet, will emerge from the old one by means of it. And you feed it by shifting your perspective, making sharp distinctions and thinking daring new thoughts. Nothing dramatic early on, though. Only this little tension from the novelty of new ideas.

Each time you understand and embrace a new idea about life inside your mind, about your emotional pain, or about what it might mean as a human to be in the present moment, you turn the barrel a little more, and a little more tension builds. Old, unexamined needs, yearnings and demands, which keep generating your painful emotions, come under the pressure of your awareness as you steadily focus on them. And if you continue to be curious and delve into the character of these dark spells coming from your brain through these negative emotions, liberating realizations can keep occurring and it can turn the whole pattern of your mind in against itself with more and more force.

The difficulty of staying with the tension inside is at the heart of why a therapist is often so necessary in order to help someone make it all the way to a breakthrough point. This tension can be very jarring. It can be downright threatening, because so much about how life has been experienced is now being questioned and challenged. The tension is what leads so many people to give up and seek an easier way to change, or to forget about the whole thing and just let time take them as it will—if it will—to more pleasant moments.

But I believe this tension is everything when it comes to a genuine breakthrough. It's not just an unavoidable side effect of the process. It's loaded with potential. It's what happens when one part of our brain (awareness) is having an encounter with another part (the limbic system), challenging its activity, having a showdown with it. This tension is the leading edge of the transformation itself; it's the very soul of the breakthrough.

And we can learn to see this discomfort as not altogether unpleasant. Compared with the anguish and futility that led to needing help in the first place, the tension we feel in the efforts we make to go against our own emotional pain, and into our unknown potential for strength, is a creative kind of tension, maybe the essence of all creativity. What encourages and inspires us as it grows is the feeling that revolutionary truths about our minds and about human existence are being realized which have the potential for becoming huge new reserves of personal power.

And so the tension in that pattern at the end of the kaleidoscope keeps building as we work with our courage and our will to turn the barrel against our own fear and deep resistance to change. The drama intensifies inside between the new and the old, the better and the worse. The line between our hope and our despair sharpens. We keep pressing and pressing further and further, trying hard to seize this moment and change how we're choosing to react to it—until the conflict between the blind force of whatever powerful emotion is pulling hard on us, and our straining efforts to resist the pull, rises to a rumbling breaking point—and then the whole tumbling pattern collapses into a new one—at least for this very moment right now—and there will be a new feeling of calm, stillness and steadiness. Like a seedling that's broken through a hard shell. Or like a butterfly that has torn open its chrysalis.

Growing pains are the beginning and the end of a breakthrough. The ultimate goal of this show is to engender a love of growing pains.

Curtain.

ACT I

The Inside of Your Mind and That Past of Yours, Particularly, those Hypnotic Thoughts that, I'm Afraid, are Forever in Revolt at the Heart of Every Single Painful Emotion

Curtain Rises

And could you keep your heart in wonder at the daily miracles of your life, your pain would not seem less wondrous than your joy.

Kahlil Gibran
The Prophet (1923)

Scene 1

What in the World is the Mind Anyway?
Does it Really Exist?
And Isn't it Mysterious?

The better to prepare you for strange truth,
Let me explain those shapes you see ahead.

Dante Alighieri
The Inferno,
The Divine Comedy (ca.1307)

Lights come up.

[*Among other things in this scene, Consciousness tries to be patient listening to Hartman.*]

Here begins all I know to help you:

So I've gazed into a few thousand human minds by now, and I've gotten a tantalizing view of what's inside. I've seen the mind's capacity for love even when it contains excruciating pain, or evil. I've seen what a storehouse of potential it is, how swiftly and cunningly it works, and how vast and daring is its reach, building thoughts that are even bigger than the universe, as it dreams and strives to handle its life.

It never stops being strange for me to see what's there. In all my training and reading, I've come across so many attempts to describe the inside of our minds and how they work. Most of the explanations sounded quaint or even hokey. They make the mind seem clunky and mechanical that, for me, takes all the life and enchantment out of it.

To me the mind is a wild thing. It lives in the wild, always stirring in its natural motion, just like the time that's ceaselessly flowing through it.

We know that our minds somehow arise from our brains. But there's so much more to a mind than a brain. Our memories have old daylight still glowing in them which once came streaming in from the light of the Sun. And the mind also comes from the eons of time that have flowed through it, sculpting it into its current shape. And it comes from whatever shimmering tides of magnetism and elementary particles are washing through it each moment. It's also made of all of the endless space inside the matter in our brains, where there's nothing at all for vast distances (on a quantum scale), and where there might be unknown places we can tear through to enter other dimensions. And the mind may also be made from something that's not matter or space or time at all.

We are being called upon now in this modern age to examine this strange old thing we're inside of, how it works, and how it can work better for us. I think it will have to become urgent, as our world coalesces, for us to focus on all of the painful emotions flaring up from inside this brain which have haunted us throughout history as individuals and are now threatening civilization by disrupting, distorting and darkening our clear view of what potential and challenges await us in our present moment, which is inside outside, and everywhere, beckoning to us, then passing away forever.

Lights down.

Scene 2

The Mind is Better than a Clock: It Doesn't Just Mark Each Moment; It Collects Them All; It Socks Them All Away.

Tell me, where all past yeares are.

John Donne (1572–1631)
Song,
The Complete Poetry and
Selected Prose of John Donne (1994)

Lights come up.

[Among other things in this scene, Consciousness continues feeling doubtful and uncomfortable, glancing out the window often, as Hartman waxes poetic about all the dignity and beauty he sees in the human mind.]

The mind is such a baffling thing to grasp. It's hard to put our finger on, because it seems to be made of time from one end to the other: it's filled with the past as visual memories and old feelings; it can experience right now through our awareness (you); and it tries to anticipate and plan for the future. Past, present, future. That's what the mind appears to be, and that's the work it appears to do.

Just as our lungs are designed to work with air, our muscles and bones with gravity, our gastrointestinal tracts with nutrients, and our immune systems with invaders, our minds seem to be designed to work with the flowing of time through our lives. But the mind is not an organ like ones made of flesh. The mind can't be made of clunky flesh if it's going to

19

maneuver through our moments of life. Instead, it needs to be like time itself, which seems to be more a flow of events than a thing like the brain. And as a kind of movement, the mind is never static, not even for one instant. Huge, silent volumes of luminous images churn and move through it in a continual metamorphosis, working hypnotic spells on us with their meanings, moving us to our feelings and actions. And because it doesn't live its life in space, the mind has that feeling of being not quite in the body. It pulses and moves around in the brain, but in a completely different realm from it. Yet the mind is solid like any other organ of the body, but solid in the way a story in a book or a piece of music is solid; it's solid with the process of time. The mind is in the brain the way the beat is in the heart.

If you want to *feel* the time inside your mind, think of a ten-year-old and a fifty-year-old. For a ten-year-old, one year is a full 10 percent of a lifetime. Time seems to pass slowly. Summers last and last. Birthdays seem far away. Waiting for anything seems to take a long time. But for the fifty-year-old, that same year is only 2 percent of a lifetime. The fifty-year-old experiences that same year as a much shorter amount of time than the ten-year-old does. Phht!—there goes another vacation, another summer, and another year. The same period of time *seems* to go so much faster for the fifty-year-old because it's a much smaller portion of all the time that has accumulated inside his or her mind. So our very experience of time has to do with how many moments we've collected in our minds. In this way, we *feel* the very substance of time that our minds are made of.

For better or worse, and out of some sort of mysterious necessity, the mind is a kind of trinity of the past, present and future.

Lights down.

Scene 3

The Basic Equipment:
Consciousness (that Means You) and the
Rest of Your Mind. Or in Other Words:
The Playgoer, the Playhouse, and the Show

The mind is its own place, and in itself
Can make a heav'n of hell, and a hell of heav'n

John Milton
Paradise Lost (1665)

Lights come up.

[*Among other things in this scene, Consciousness, straight faced, serious, notices how taken Hartman is with everything in theater, and all the theater in every move we make.*]

Aren't our minds a lot like theaters, playhouses, in which there is always a show going on as the time of our lives keeps flowing? The playgoer is awareness. And the show is all of the perceptions, thoughts, feelings and images evoked in our minds that we weave into the grand and deep meaning of our human existence.

Before I became a psychologist, I made the mistake of assuming that my entire mind was just one pure, single thing: mind. That was it. It was all in one space and seemed to be of one piece. But as I think about something or someone, imagine something, or recall a memory, it becomes obvious that my mind is not one thing, but two. Like a moviegoer and the movie, they are distinct from each other. Each is somehow animated by its own kind of

21

energy and purpose, yet they're also both deeply connected and in an intimate relationship with one another.

Our dear Consciousness—the playgoer or moviegoer—you are that sense of awareness hovering somewhere behind our eyes, poised at the threshold of two worlds: the one inside our minds and the one outside, and living in that colossal crack of light called the present moment, between all the time that has passed and all that lies ahead. And although awareness seems to be just a faint little nebula inside, it's somehow loaded with the substance of our character: intuitions, morals, values, principles, beliefs, and our will. It has the ability to experience and engage our whole person in the world, to stir memory, to fantasize and imagine, to think and be inspired.

And then there's the show inside our minds. As the present moment passes away, our awareness parts with what it has experienced, which then strangely falls away deep into our minds becoming a memory—the raw footage of our own independent films. As long as we live, we're always parting ways with the moments of our lives as they collect and drift inside our minds, in the state of potential called memory, while our awareness goes on to encounter the next one.

So our memories and imaginings become something different from us, from our awareness. They came from our intimate experience with Now, but when we let them loose into our minds, they become a very different substance from us. We part ways with what we've experienced, and it remains there inside our minds for at least the rest of our lives.

This is the basic equipment in our minds: our awareness along with all of our archived thoughts and feelings, snapshots, scenes, movies, plays. But there is also something else to show you still deeper down inside our brain which we will all need to reckon with well so that we can go on peacefully.

Lights down.

Scene 4

Is It an Emergency for Us to Realize Certain Things About Our Own Minds and Our Lives, Or What?

Seeing is in some respects an art that must be learnt.

William Herschel (1738–1822)
British astronomer

Lights come up.

[*Among other things in this scene, Consciousness notices the intensity and ambition in Hartman's green eyes.*]

So many people say this to me: "I don't think I really need a therapist or therapy. I *know* what's wrong with me. And I know what I have to do about it."

Yeah? So what about *doing* it? Where does that part come in? How do you get up the strength and the will to *do* it?

Or people say this:

"Give me a tool ( ).

That's what I need ( ).

I need a tool to help me ( )."

And what they're actually saying is this:

"Give me a tool (so it could be easy).

That's what I need (so it could be very easy).

I need a tool to help me (so it could be easy, like magic)."

Well, I have a tool that works. It won't be like magic, though. Because self-esteem doesn't, can't ever, grow out of magic. No, this tool is called *realization*.

We have this dark dilemma on our hands called emotional pain, and it's urgent for us to learn how to do something about it for the sake of each person and the world. I declare that painful emotions affect us like very powerful spells that flare up from the depths of our minds, our brains, and engulf us while we're trying to take care of our business in the here and now. To break these dark spells as they flare, or even before they flare, we need to learn how to light up the inside of our minds by setting off flashes in there which I'm calling realizations. And we need to set off enough of them to awaken us quickly from these spells when they threaten to take hold and cause their havoc.

There have been enough wise men and women who've walked the earth to know that it can be done. And our troubles are getting harder and harder to hide. Coming out of these spells needs to be done by more than just a few wise men and women. Our species could use a regular revolution in mind health. Mental and emotional health ought to be as plentiful as bread. Once upon a time, there weren't many loaves of bread, either.

So we need to learn how to *realize*, like the sages have. And I mean realize the very simplest things right under our noses, and right behind our noses. I'm talking about seeing and appreciating very deeply that there's this thing called a mind, that it's made of and deals with events and the passage of time. And inside this theater of our mind is our own precious, maturing awareness (you), perhaps 200,000 years old, though the huge enhancement to consciousness of civilization is only about 14,000 years old. And then deeper down in our brain is what's called our limbic system, possibly 150 million years old, currently threatening our emotional health and the survival of our species. Finally, there is also this other urgently important thing, like bold theater lights, called Now.

By realization, I don't mean simply knowing about something. Realization is like a little celebration in our minds. Like a birthday party with hats, cake and candles. Hooray! you're here right before my eyes! Realization is a special way of appreciating the existence of something. It can take you all the way to the heart of something, like the pain in your mind or a star deep in space, and allow you at the same time to be far away from it and safe, but stronger for the knowing. Realizations don't have to strike you haphazardly in life, like lightning from above. They can be tools you use, like wattage in light bulbs, to light up your mind and find your way.

And you make realizations grow like muscles in a gym that can be flexed at will. And when these muscles happen to be the ones in the wings of your awareness, they become the way you travel from the depths of those awful spells, called painful emotions and bad moods, all the way back to Now. Then you can involve yourself more comfortably in your efforts to achieve the attainable, or just become supremely enchanted by the simplest of things.

You're with me now in the gym to build realizations. One-two, one-two. I'm like a personal trainer or a coach to help build realizations. One-two, one-two. And for the sake of the world and for each of us, growing these muscles may be a matter of survival. One-two. This young thing in our brain, only 200,000 years old at most, and only 14,000 years in a big way, taking on another part of our brain that's 150 million years old and always battle-ready. One-two, one-two, one-two…

Lights down.

Scene 5

A Preview of a Fantastic Mass of Moments Inside Our Brains Where All, I Tell You, All of Our Emotional Pain Comes from

What is your substance, whereof are you made,
That millions of strange shadows on you tend?

William Shakespeare
Sonnet 53 (1609)
The Complete Works of William Shakespeare (2007)

Lights come up.

[*Among other things in this scene, Consciousness thinks about Hartman's mind being in the stars, and what kind of trouble he might have had as a dreamy, quiet kid.*]

The movies playing inside the theaters of our minds are where we go to realize the truths about our emotional pain. And through the mind we can get right to the brain.

When we look inside, what we see phosphorescing back to life are the scenes we've lived and imagined: part snapshot, part motion picture. Each image we find there broke away from our experience of life—some present moment we were in—and mysteriously took a little of our awareness with it. Moment by moment, time slowly, quietly, and relentlessly disperses us into our pasts as memories, old thoughts and imaginings.

Direct your attention to another time in your life, and you can feel the gentle surging of your will as it moves around in the fertile spaces of your mind, breeze-like, feeling for different moments of your life, stirring up images the way a wind can stir up piles of leaves. The images you come up with swirl back to life, flash slowly and vividly, linger for a while, and then fall away, mysteriously linked with you, mysteriously you.

There are all kinds of collections of these images warehoused inside. And whatever it is we remember seems to be an exact reproduction of the actual moment of time we experienced, although it's uncertain whether it may have undergone some kind of alteration since its original imprint, even what we experienced just moments ago. But they're all that's left of the flashing moments of our lives in this world. And they live on inside our minds, glowing more softly with the energy of hidden feeling and meaning.

Many therapist work with these collections of images and scenes, treating them like great works of literature and art. They mine them for the deepest meaning in the painful dilemmas of early life and try to see how they are interfering with our fulfillment in the present: the way we once loved and needed love, how we felt sorrows and joys, how we expressed them or hid them from others, and where, in those troubled scenes in our lives, our potential for growth lies frozen. Many therapists believe strongly that these images—the scenes and movies inside—are the passageways to our deepest secrets, and most importantly of all, to our transformation.

I also believe this is true and a valid way to work. But because my head has always been more in the stars, and less in words and stories, I've also been drawn to another kind of past inside that's different from these movie-like, visual memories. I've been drawn to something I keep seeing there in each person I work with, something dark and suspended heavily there amid all the lighted imagery.

This thing I see is not made of pictures. It's strangely alive and very concentrated in one place, and it speaks with a voice that's silent but potent, like the force of gravity. It has primitive reserves of strength and works a painful, deadly magic upon us. It pulls on us because it (often mistakenly) senses danger and becomes frightened. It tugs as a wish; it pulls harder on us as a yearning; or it wrenches like a demand. It pulls awareness down inside and back in time, and sometimes very far away from right now.

And the needing this thing does often has little to do with actual necessities, with the need for oxygen, food, water, friendship, or the achievement of a goal. Rather, what it needs, urgently and immediately, is the most perfect love and security there could be.

Each of us humans has one of these things to reckon with inside our brains. No exceptions. This is our limbic system.

And this little description I've just given you is only a preview of this entity inside our minds. There are more details to come. This distressed tissue in our brains is full of huge power and influence. I believe it's what's responsible for all of our emotional pain, from the slightest feelings of irritation and annoyance all the way to the wildest storms of rage, panic, depression and misery, not to mention violence and war.

The first thing I try to get a person to do is just "see" it, to sense it there inside—one part of the brain sensing the activity of another part. This might take some time, though. As I go along in my work, I keep trying to permanently change the way a person views emotional pain. Instead of seeing it as a justified reaction we have to the way we're being treated by the world, I keep urging people to entertain the possibility that our reaction is actually flaring, in a fantastic sort of way, out of this strange mass of old feeling *inside* our minds, our brains. Our pain is made of our past in a fantastic way, with the power to pull us way off course. And, fantastically enough, it often doesn't have anything at all to do with whatever is going on out there right now. Our whole reaction is nothing more than a kind of choice we are making, or rather a choice being made for us by that old thing flaring up, responding with its old, dark emotion from a former time.

I find that we strengthen ourselves against it simply by seeing it and continuing to see and realize what it is saying, and how wrong its assessment often is of our reality. With the help of certain guiding truths about it, we can hold our gaze still, through all of its fantastic gusts of enchantment and disenchantment, and finally break its spell over us. And when we can do this, and it will take time to do, we will have broken free from the grip of the past and can have an encounter with the unexpected, mysterious nature of this present moment right now ...

Lights down.

Scene 6

The Present Moment. This Very Instant. Now! (It's Everything to Us. Well, Almost Everything.)

I think of this in terms of the sea, in the image of the sea as it breaks upon the shore. It is not the wave that comes, it is the whole sea that comes each time and the whole sea that draws back. It is never just a wave, it is always everything that comes and everything that goes.

Edmond Jabes, French author,
interviewed by Paul Auster in
The Art of Hunger (1978)

Lights come up.

[*Among other things in this scene, Hartman thinks about how innocent Consciousness is just sitting there listening, taking it all in, and about all the difficult, fateful work that needs to be done.*]

Now is the main event in our lives. It's where all the action is, where we love and do our work, where we live and die.

That segment of time we call "Now" seems like it's just the smallest part of our lifetime. But it's not small. If we lift the idea of it out of the ordinary flow of life—where it tends to dissolve so quickly into concerns about the past and future—and if we look at it as an entity by itself, it begins to look like a huge miracle. It's immovable and indestructible, materializing continuously out of nowhere. This all-embracing interval of time, seeming to hold all the starlight and sunlight and the light of civilization and everything in stillness or motion—all of it, all at once—floods into our minds, sculpting us continuously with its impact.

29

Now is so distinct a presence and yet so elusive. It's not just another moment of time. It's really our only actual one. According to physicists there is no such thing as an encompassing present moment, but rather a profusion of them, because of the infinitesimally different lengths of time it takes light to travel to our eyes from between all of the objects participating in what we're calling the present moment. But psychologically we can speak of the event of a present moment. There is this strong sense of cohesion in the way we each experience our own existence—we continue, through the passage of time, to be distinctly one thing to ourselves—and so we might naturally impart that same sense of cohesion to other things and to moments, like the one around us. And maybe we can feel so exhilaratingly alive in this moment because what we think of as a single present moment is actually this multiplicity, this chorus of instants singing out to us and lighting us up.

And it might seem we could make Now reappear or echo in our memory, but it's vastly different from any memory we can have of it. Memories are partial and come and go, but Now is all-encompassing and will never leave us for as long as we live. Even all our memories can only be recalled in the light of Now.

For whatever mysterious reasons, our universe coalescences for us into these present moment events, each one dramatic as a stage play, each containing everything there is. And Now is ultimate and final, like conception and death. You spend your entire life in it. It's not a creation of our minds; it's a display of nature, like light and motion and matter. We have no choice but to experience it. It's ever-present and all-pervasive. It's what connects us to other humans and to the rest of the cosmos. Now contains everything there is, was, and ever will be.

Almost everything, that is. Our negative, painful emotions are antagonistic to Now. Now, along with our awareness, is what these emotions flare so hard against. They seek in their dark magic and fierceness to obliterate any obstacle in their way in order to fulfill the old primitive yearning in our brain to be safe. Under the spell of a painful emotion our awareness can be pulled far away from Now, and persuades us to believe that it shouldn't exist at all, that a better one should be there, a perfect one.

Lights down.

Scene 7

Ladies and Gentlemen, Human Emotional Pain is Truly Amazing. It's One of the Wonders of the Natural World. Watch It Completely Reject the Present Moment Right Before Your Eyes. Just Like That!

In the fight between you and the world, back the world.

Franz Kafka
The Great Wall of China (1946)

Lights come up.

[*Among other things in this scene, Consciousness is restless, stirring and shifting around often in the chair, making it rock and bob up and down a little throughout the scene. Hartman notes the restlessness with amusement.*]

From the strange core of our emotional pain deep inside, made from our past, a cry of rejection—*No!*—rises up into the present moment at the surface of our lives to take on the obstacles we encounter there.

Choose any emotion on the list of painful emotions (scene 9). Annoyance, frustration, anger, fear, etc. Watch the feeling flare up in the slowest motion, and watch it reject what's happening right now. When you're blending hopelessly into a major traffic jam on the only possible road you can take to get to where you need to go in a hurry—*No!*; or when you're on the telephone trying to negotiate an impenetrable phone menu to get important information or to undo a potentially damaging or costly

31

error made against you—*No!*; or when someone you thought you knew better treats you with outrageous insensitivity—*No!*; or when you encounter anything at all that thwarts you—a feeling of dismay begins to gather and press inside, saying—*No!* The negative emotion may subside as you accept your situation and settle into it. Or it might flare in ever stronger waves with each assessment you make of the situation.

When I begin to work with someone who's in one sort of emotional pain or another, the very first way I hear this pain is as a blunt cry of rejection—rejection of what's going on in life, rejection of reality, of Now. I ask myself, "How much of Now is being rejected here?" The answer comes in the form of a kind of magnitude, an amount that I sense. This is how I begin to size up the power of that mass of old feeling in a person's mind, the ferocity of the limbic system in his or her brain. It has a kind of voice that cries out each time we're thwarted. It says, to one degree or another, "What's going on right now should not be going on. It's not acceptable. Something more desirable should be happening now instead of this."

Our limbic system basically says "No!" to events in life that aren't ideal and satisfying. It rejects them, and blames them for withholding fulfillment, ease, or pleasure. Or it rejects and blames us for not doing more about a world that's being so disappointing and difficult. The more thwarted we are, the more intense the pain in our minds can become, and the more scathing the rejection and blame. It's as though the source of pain in our minds is having a tantrum. It's engaged in a childlike effort to get rid of the event.

But the truth is that trying to reject an event that's taking place right now also means trying to get rid of the present moment the event is embedded in, too. And that means trying to get rid of the rest of the universe. Because events, the present moment, and the rest of the universe are all profoundly interconnected and inseparable from one another. If you try to get rid of one of them, you have to get rid of all of them, and then everything goes. This is very hard to realize *while* the pain is flaring. But this is the goal. And this is where the breakthrough point is.

A great personal tragedy occurs when emotional pain flares into awareness and we're not strong enough to resist it. The primitive cry of "No!" our pain utters in its innocent effort to solve the problem before us can be overpowering. What it's doing is demanding something the present moment does not and cannot contain. We humans have a unique and fantastic ability for desiring this thing, and it explains why we can suffer so: *What the present moment cannot ever contain is the instantaneous replacement of itself with another, more preferable, more satisfying, more perfect moment simply because we wish, expect or demand that it were so.* So within each negative painful emotion there's this insistent magical wish for this present moment, along with its circumstances, to be replaced by a different one. This is the impossible paradox in our magical thinking and the dilemma of our species.

It would be wonderful to create a new kind of present moment. And it can be visionary when we're prepared to make all of the strenuous efforts necessary to build one. But we can become paralyzed emotionally and cease to function when we demand a different moment to magically materialize before us, instantaneously, without any effort on our part. This is what emotional pain does—in short bursts in everyday life, or in the more ravaging bouts that may strike us in more difficult times. In the throes of emotional pain, we don't want the world we have and we don't have the world we want. In our emotional pain, however slight, we don't really have any world at all, so we suffer a little or a lot.

When we can believe these two facts—that when the source of painful emotions inside our minds is flaring up it is rejecting reality (the present moment and everything in it, including our awareness), and, that this source of emotions is an entirely different entity from awareness, a completely different part of the anatomy of our own brain— these facts become two of the most catalytic realizations we could have about life, and can pave the way for the paradigm shift that I'm calling a breakthrough: the shift from the limbic system's sense of things dominating our lives and the world to Consciousness being in charge.

So, painful emotion is there flaring inside our minds. But it's different from awareness. It flares up from a different part of our brain. And it operates by a drastically different kind of logic. This very idea is a difficult one to believe because of how indivisible our minds can *feel* moment to moment. It's difficult to believe that our pain is coming from what is practically another source of life inside our minds. But it does. And that's our great hope.

So I listen very carefully to the way emotional pain is "speaking" and rejecting the world. I try to determine to what degree a person's awareness is in agreement with it, and how vulnerable it is to its influence. I also try to find out how much a person might be capable of believing that his or her awareness is different from the pain, and how motivated he or she might be to disagree with the demands and the rejection of the world that are flaring up from it, and be able to break free. The power of pain to enchant us into believing it and agreeing with it can be awesome. It sweeps through us, taking us over before we know it. And it has been flaring up in us humans for eons.

And this is why it's not enough to read in a book or hear someone say, "Just be in the moment." How is it possible to just let go of what is completely overpowering you and has you so tightly in its grip? It's like saying, "Just disregard that person who's strangling you, who has you by the throat and is threatening your life. Just enjoy the beauty of the moment."

No, to break the grip of emotional pain—the quick, momentary flaring of it, or the more prolonged, wrenching bouts—requires more than just thinking positively. It'll involve *realizing* that the menace is there—*seeing* the menace—and by *seeing* deeply and powerfully enough, throwing it off, and breaking free of its hold. And we'll have to use all our might—at first, anyway.

*   *   *

So how many times a day does one painful emotion or another flare up inside your mind?

And how long does each flaring emotion last? Moments? Minutes? Hours? Years?

And tell me, what kind of toll does it take on you? On your mind and your spirit? And on your body?

And imagine, how much of this goes on in a lifetime? In all the lifetimes of all the people who have ever lived?

Lights down.

Scene 8

Doubts About Any of This?
Or All of This?

Will you, won't you, will you, won't you, will you join the dance?

Lewis Carroll
Alice's Adventures in
Wonderland (1865)

Lights come up.

[*Among other things in this scene, Consciousness and Hartman smile subtly at each other with their doubts.*]

I'm in my office at the beginning of another session, looking at the person sitting on the middle cushion of my couch. A woman. She's lean with tight, wavy dark hair, pretty facial features, dark blue eyes, and very strong convictions. She can be engaging. She can smile and laugh, telling me about a man she's dated, an incident at work, or the goings-on in her family. But she is admittedly lost in a pain, wanting so much to find the right person to spend her life with, but afraid she never will. So strong are her doubts, she's afraid of making any changes at all because of what might never happen.

As she begins to speak, those depths and distances in a person's mind make themselves felt in me again, as they do in each of us, whenever another mind comes close and begins to open. From far off inside, out of the vanishing point of her ancestry and the world of her childhood, come the patterns of speech, the mannerisms, and the vulnerabilities of her family, which she renders in her ironic, ardent way of speaking, and in the way her mood respectfully warms and cools as our time together passes.

36

My crucial tasks are to spot her awareness—to spot *her*—and try to see how much *she* gets caught up in the gravitational pull of those little orbs in her limbic system called her amygdalae, dense with fear and yearning, anchored there in stereo on either side deep in her brain. My task is also to find out how well she can maneuver out of their hypnotic grip. Moment by moment, I try to assess what work will need to be done with her so *she* can pull herself free from her own pain and feel good about herself and her life.

All the years have made it easier for me to see these things inside and to work with them. But I still contend with the echoes of old doubts I had about psychology before I entered the field, doubts that much of the world still has, and doubts she has, too.

When I'm absorbed in looking at what's in her mind, the inside is all open: it's panoramic, endless, and filled with reason and rhyme. There are the sounds of her life, the evocation of her worlds, the ways *she* reaches inside her mind for imagery and expression to secure her meaning and to share it with me. And there is the quiet, painful grip of those yearnings to be loved.

But when the session ends and she leaves my office, the whole interior of her mind goes completely out. What animates her disappears. My fix on her is gone. I have to admit to myself that I won't have any sense at all about what's going on in her until next time. I can only surmise and wonder from the flickering of afterimages in my own mind.

The mind is not an object that can be captured in a scan, like the folds of the brain, and viewed at one's leisure. It's made out of the flowing of time, like a piece of music. So we have to let it play in time, and listen and see, to know what's there. And when our time with it is interrupted, it seems to vanish altogether and cease to exist, like a song when it stops. This is what it must be like for everyone, and even more dismissively for those who don't appreciate the vastness and complexity there is inside a person's mind. It's easy to doubt that what's in the mind is really there at all.

All of psychology once seemed to me to be just matters of opinion, like anything we can't put our finger on. Descriptions I read long ago of the mind always made it sound too hypothetical, or too mystical, or too much a spirit world to be such a significant part of ordinary, day-to-day life. This is why I once doubted and disliked psychology so much.

That was once. But I do relive my doubts now and then as their echoes get evoked in my mind, like harmonics, by the same doubts in everyone I work with.

And there's still another, stranger doubt I have about this work. I do believe I'm actually seeing what's there in someone's mind. What I see there feels as real to me as the night sky. But it all seems to be going on in a non-physical, subjective medium. So I wonder sometimes if what I see hovering there in another person's mind are only patterns lighting up in my brain, ignited by my curiosity—that what I'm looking at so intently in someone else is really only myself.

But none of these doubts interfere with or weaken the work. They may even enhance it by strengthening my focus on why I'm doing it. I'm not just seeing what's inside for the sake of seeing, as interesting as that can be. And I didn't come to these views I hold by daydreaming about them. They came from so many moments spent with people trying to figure out how to help them change, how to create a way to steady a mind in pain and produce a calmer way to react to the tumult of life.

And it doesn't matter anymore if what I see and do is ultimately scientifically verifiable by anyone else or not. Because when it's very important to the people in my office to change their awareness, and when I find the simplest and most vivid words, timed as carefully as I can to convey what I see inside, and I negotiate the natural reluctance to let go of old ways and embrace new ones, it helps set off wonderful transformations, small or large, time after time.

Lights down.

Scene 9

And Now, Ladies and Gentlemen, For Your Entertainment Pleasure, Introducing Our Painful Emotions ...

Sadness does not inhere in things; it does not reach us from the world and through mere contemplation of the world. It is a product of our own thought. We create it.

Emile Durkheim
Suicide (1897)

Lights come up.

[Among other things in this scene, Consciousness is a tiny bit amused riding the rainbow of painful emotions.]

And here is what I mean by painful emotions. Each one on the following list comes flaring up from a source deep inside our minds as we try to live our lives in the present moment. At their very best, these feelings could serve as great signals to us of obstacles we're encountering in our world. The problem with them is not that we feel them at all, but how long we feel them, how intensely, and how much they can ravage our functioning. Understanding these feelings in the way I'll propose is not to eliminate them so that we never feel them again, but to regulate them, to develop a new relationship with them so that we might be able to affect their intensity and not be so blindsided and dominated by them, and maybe even be free of them completely for long periods.

Each time one of these emotions sweeps through us is another chance to understand its workings deep inside our minds, where our past lives, where old struggles and pain are preserved in deep deposits and networks of old feeling on either side of our brain, which is also known, in this moment in history, as our limbic system—the connected areas in our brain concerned with self preservation in the face of threats to life. We can listen carefully as feelings flare from it and we can translate its strange old language. And when we can build the strength to see it and listen to it straight on, without flinching, as it threatens to overpower us, we can have that catalytic experience, so necessary for a lasting change, called realization or insight. We can realize what it means to be a human with a past, a primitive past, still so alive inside our minds, a past that can feel more powerfully and hauntingly alive to us than what is right before us. And we can realize, as we hold our gaze steadily on it and listen and grasp what it is actually saying to us, how urgent it is to pull ourselves free from its innocent, well-meaning but relentlessly frantic grip.

Each and every time we experience one of these emotions, we have yet another opportunity to stage a breakthrough.

Irritation
Impatience
Annoyance
Exasperation
Frustration
Resentment
Anger
Animosity
Aversion
Disgust
Fury
Hatred
Contempt
Disdain
Cynicism
Jealousy
Envy
Greed
Bitterness

Futility
Weariness
Boredom
Emptiness
Loneliness
Insecurity
Anxiety
Worry
Apprehension
Dread
Fear
Helplessness
Desperation
Panic
Bewilderment
Bafflement
Disappointment
Discouragement
Regret
Dejection
Inadequacy
Guilt
Embarrassment
Shame
Humiliation
Sadness
Gloom
Desolation
Depression
Hopelessness
Despair
Despondency
Torment
Misery

Lights down.

Scene 10

And Here, Ladies and Gentlemen, are the Ways We Experience Our Painful Emotions …

One is cured of a suffering only by experiencing it to the full.

Marcel Proust
In Search of Lost Time (1925)

Lights come up.

[*Among other things in this scene, Consciousness listens to each line as though Hartman is singing a song.*]

Painful emotions seem to have followed our first breath, as though they came from our exposure to the world. As children, we struggle with them. Because they hurt so much, we secretly and urgently try to make sense of these emotions and try to come up with a solution to relieve ourselves of them and avert their sting. And so, early in our childhoods we each devise a master plan to avoid all of the pain the world seems to be causing by striving to be perfect and live perfect lives.

But until we can go inside our own minds to the heart of the pain itself and have our showdown with it, we're sure to feel it again and again no matter how perfect we try to be. We won't be able to avert it, avoid it, or relieve ourselves of it no matter what we do, yet we keep following our plan because we know of no other.

It's a great flaw in our thinking, originating in our innocence as children, that it's the world that brings us the pain. By the time we reach adulthood, we may not even think twice about this. We just assume our pain comes from our contact with the world:

The pain of chaos and confusion, and the need for someone or something to be there.

The pain of being ignored

The pain of the dark

The pain of criticism when you need so much to be supported and soothed

The pain of thinking, "I'm not enough"

Of knowing how much love you have and how little it's appreciated

Of loneliness

Of time moving too slowly

Of boredom

The pain of not knowing the answer to a question

The pain of getting frustrated for needing what seems so reasonable

The pain of not feeling smart enough

Or cultured enough

Or athletic enough

Or creative enough

Or attractive enough

Or acceptable

The pain of being able to see the beauty in someone and being rejected anyway

The pain of fighting angrily through a strong wind to get somewhere

Of rushing so we could be somewhere

Of being kept waiting for a very long time

The pain of uncertainty

The pain of being involved with someone who doesn't want your relationship to go any deeper or be any more permanent

The pain of being heartbroken again and again and not understanding why

The pain of the way your face looks

Or your body

The pain of being looked at and not seen

Of not having enough money

Of having enough money but not having enough money

The pain of a physical deformity

The pain in a relationship with a parent
The pain of disappointment in human nature
Of traffic jams
Of having your time wasted
The pain of always needing to win, even when there's no real contest
The pain of parting ways with a friend
The pain of thinking less of people
Of knowing how much corruption there is
Of dreary weather persisting for weeks
Of not even liking a sunny day in the summertime
The pain of realizing how little we really know about anything
Of not enough sex
Of not enough free time
Of how hard it is to lose weight
Of living next door to the wrong person
Of needing a kind of car that makes you feel like something
The pain of too much of the wrong kind of work to do
The pain of your child having an illness or being in pain
Of realizing that positive thinking doesn't work that well
Of realizing how fast time is moving
And of how much of life has gone by
The pain of seeing how much more someone else has: more talent, more beauty, more money, more of everything
The pain of realizing that, barring the wildly unexpected, you may not have the wealth or the achievement you once dreamed of
The pain of too much responsibility
The pain of learning that someone you know died suddenly
The pain of watching someone you know die slowly
The pain of worrying about something terrible happening
Of a terrorist attack
Or a hurricane
Or an earthquake
Or a flood
Or a car crash

The pain of too much stress too often

The pain of a diagnosis of cancer

Of having had cancer

Of worrying

The pain of yearning for security in a world where there's very little, and it's fleeting

The pain of realizing how much pain there is in the world

The pain of realizing you might not have enough faith that the problems in the world will work themselves out

The pain of thinking about your children dealing with this world, and without you

The pain of apprehension about what's to come

The pain of yearning for a solution that's not at hand

The pain of yearning for relief

The pain of yearning

Lights down.

Scene 11

And Last but not Least, Ladies and Gentlemen, Here are the Ways We Express Our Painful Emotions …

I tell you one must harbor chaos
if one would give birth to a dancing star.

Friedrich Nietzsche
Thus Spake Zarathustra (1892)

Lights come up.

[Among other things in this scene, Consciousness notices again Hartman's love of high drama.]

Negative feelings have a tenacity to them that seems to suggest they've been with us for eons and are deeply entwined with our nature. Despite our bursts of ingenuity and our ability to create the most moving and breath-taking beauty, we humans keep going through the centuries struggling with the *pain* of negative feelings. It's easy to wonder whether this *pain* is so basic to being alive and human, and so elusive and tricky in its ways, that we might go on struggling with it, in the way we have been, forever.

In my work, I get to see from up close how psychological *pain* has grown in a person, how deeply its roots go, and how it branches so quietly through a person's mind, sending fracture lines through a life as it goes. Most of the time we just harbor our *pain* and find ways to live in spite of it. Sometimes the fracture lines grow large enough to break us apart.

Whenever our *pain* is even slightly stronger than our awareness, it'll be impossible to keep it hidden. It'll strain the melody in your voice and make your face tense. It'll estrange you from all the beauty there is inside and out. It'll drain the light right out of your eyes.

And *pain* can drive the life out of our solitude. It can send us into secret, forbidden places where we try to control the *pain*, or at least achieve some distraction from it for a while.

And *pain* jars relationships, jamming humans together in conflict, or into unsound dependencies, and then driving them apart in futility. It may determine a career choice or a choice of spouse. Twinges of *pain* may regularly go jolting through families, ricocheting among its members and shooting out into the community. Then it seeps relentlessly down into yet another generation.

And there's that definite but elusive algebra, which we can sense at times but not prove quite yet, between emotional *pain* in the mind and chronic and deadly illnesses in the body ... Between emotional *pain* in a person and money: salary levels, debt levels, and the way the oceans of wealth move around in the world ... Between emotional *pain* and the way an ethnic group could be discriminated against or annihilated ... Between emotional *pain* in a people and the way governments behave: the alliances they make, and their wars.

Lights down.

Scene 12

And the Cure, Ladies and Gentlemen, is
Extremely Simple but Extremely Radical—
All We Have to Do is Morph Our
Consciousness into a Big Giant Pause.
In Other Words We Need to
Learn to See and See and See
and See and Keep Seeing.
That's all there is to it.

The greatest thing a human soul ever does in this world is to see...
To see clearly is poetry, philosophy, and religion—all in one.

John Ruskin
Modern Painters (1856)

Lights come up.

[*Among other things in this scene, Consciousness daydreams about having no
real interest in seeing too deeply into anything sometimes, no matter what's at
stake.*]

Let's admit it, despite the mysterious strength holding civilization together,
humanity has big psychological problems. Feelings of pain, like the ones on
the list in scene 9, flare up way too strongly and last far too long for the
situations in life that evoke them. They ravage our individual lives, our
society and world affairs.

My practice of psychotherapy and my own personal therapy have convinced me that the extent to which we habitually experience these emo-

tions is not just a natural part of the human condition we have to resign ourselves to. It only seems that way because the urgency to do something about them is just not widely felt yet in our culture. So we humans go on succumbing way too often to the strange influence of that inflamed yearning inside our minds for some kind of magic to happen. And if it doesn't happen, we use time as an escape portal and yearn our way to a sweeter moment, away from the pain, in a troubled search for that sweetness, through distractions, purchases, mischief. But alas, the magic doesn't come to us, and when we flee into the next moment, the rest of our mind goes with us. Soon the same old painful emotions will flare again, containing the same old yearning for the magic.

And when we're strained by our negative feelings into more painful states, none of the easy, well-intended advice we get from the media teaches us nearly enough to solve the problems caused by these feelings—as everyone who seeks a solution there eventually discovers. There just isn't a complete enough picture or method there to inspire and shape the radical effort we need to change our awareness and our lives.

Nothing seems to work, even the best psychotherapy sometimes, because of how ingrained our belief is that the outside world is the problem, and how persistently we just want to be given the solution to it. On the surface, we *think* and *believe* we want to make the necessary efforts to take that journey all the way to a real change. But actually making the efforts is another matter. What I tend to see in my practice (and in myself) is that if the transit through a personal transformation were a journey by car, we'd not only want to be given the gasoline and the roadmap for the journey, we'd also like a chauffeur if we could get one.

For a dramatic change to happen, we don't only need to *want* to make the effort, but we have to actually *do* a radical thing with the effort. And the only thing that will work in any lasting way *is* the radical thing. Which is not to just be given the solution, but *to transform our very awareness into it.* Instead of just falling away from stressful moments back into the painful grip of feelings from the past and the troubled states of mind they put us in, what we need to learn to do is create a *pause*, to stop the action of succumbing to negative feelings. We turn our awareness into a *pause*, a pure, sturdy *pause* that protects us from the emotion. We're aware of it flaring, but we can keep it at bay, hold it in check, and prevent it from becoming one with us.

This pause we create helps to hold us steady in the present moment. And we can learn to sustain this pause with our will and slow down the whole experience of our inner life and all the jarring effects the negative emotion is having. And while we're pausing we can realize and grasp all the absurd things the negative feeling is saying to us: its dark rejection of the world and its lame old yearning for a different one. Then we can see, calmly and freely, what's going on out there in the universe right now: all of the limitations we need to take into consideration and all of the real possibilities.

And then all of those cute, quick, magic-sounding solutions we read or hear about will no longer appeal to us. We'll know how to morph ourselves into the right-sized pause. Not a once-and-for-all pause; just one that works for the moment. It'll feel like flexing an important muscle just the right amount in order to lift and hold something in the air.

Whenever we can turn ourselves into this pause in the face of our difficult emotions, particularly the first time, we have achieved that dramatic, liberating experience I'm referring to as a breakthrough. Just like how it must have felt when we were able to walk for the first time, holding ourselves up, *pausing* up there in the air on our own legs, knowing we're doing it and that we did it.

And then we'll know that this large, sturdy pause we can create inside our own mind *is* the answer. It's the only lasting answer there is. With practice, the experience can be repeated, preventing whatever painful emotion may threaten to take us away from the present moment. We'll be able to handle more of what's happening in our lives, or just enjoy the stillness and be astonished by it all.

Changing how we are in the world, being able to pause inside our minds, is one of the most practical things a human could ever do. But it's radical. It's little known to civilization and hard to do. Because of what we have to *see* inside and what will happen to us along the way, developing the power to build this pause and make it happen again and again, will take time and effort and courage. It's a dramatic metamorphosis. We'll need to disconnect from the world in a way and make a kind of inward movement with new ideas about our minds. We'll have to cocoon with ourselves as we deepen our involvement with the problem and the ideas.

It's very tricky to describe a change in us before it happens. I don't mean just having a moving, inspiring experience with a cleansing wash of tears, though this may happen along the way. The change I'm referring to will transform the very awareness we have right now into another kind of awareness. The old version of us won't quite be there anymore, the way the caterpillar is no longer really there in the butterfly. It's still the same animal, but it's transformed and has a very different kind of existence.

It's the same with trying to describe a new kind of awareness to an old kind of awareness. It's hard to see because the very thing that sees is transformed and disappears. It's replaced by a new thing that sees differently.

So we turn our eyes from the world outside, to the one *inside*, on our way to the strangely designed sources of painful emotions on either side of our brain deep *inside*.

Lights down.

Scene 13

Are You Ready to **See** this Thing Inside Your Mind? It's Awesome! It's Out of this World! It's Practically Celestial!

The readiness is all.

William Shakespeare
Hamlet (1601)

How to Begin to Understand One Single Painful Emotion

Lights come up.

[Among other things in this scene, Consciousness notices, along with the birds flitting around outside, how much Hartman is trying to make all of this very scientific.]

A review of the basic information:

Our mind lives in what seems a different dimension from our brain. It is the organ in our bodies that's filled with and concerned about time. Memories from the past, perceptions and thoughts in the present, and plans and imaginings about the future—all have to do with time flowing into our minds and being deposited there, forming the invisible substance of our inner worlds and our personalities. Our brain is liquid, tissue, molecules, and electricity; but our mind is time.

Besides all of the swirling imagery inside our brain, there are <u>two</u> other <u>remarkable entities</u> there. One is <u>awareness</u> (you), somehow holding miraculously steady inside for a lifetime. What awareness does is take notice; it sees what's inside and outside. It's the source of our will; it sees and decides how to respond; if and when. The other striking entity inside our brain, especially when it comes to our problems in life, also made of time like everything else in there, is the heavy source of painful emotions—our limbic system with its amygdalae—of which I'm steadily building a grand picture for you here in Act I. This other entity doesn't communicate in a visual way, like all the illuminated imagery inside. After working with this amazing thing all these years, it still holds so much mystery for me, like an object in deep space. It seems so strangely composed, such a tightly compressed and potent accumulation of certain moments collected in our brain from the distant past. And it produces all of our intense negative emotions that can either pull on us fast and hard and upset us in a sharp way, or pull more quietly and steadily, and influence us more insidiously through our mood.

When I listen to a person in emotional pain, I sense the person's awareness stuck in the grip of a feeling or feelings: *helplessness* over a child's behavior; *dread* about a disturbing physical symptom; *worry* about a financial problem; *disappointment* over events at work, or any feeling on the list. These painful emotions can tyrannize awareness. They can take us over and pull us under unproductive, disabling or dangerous hypnotic spells—momentary ones (impatience, frustration, anger), or prolonged and more ravaging ones (depression).

I believe that all we need to do to set into motion a lively transformation of the inside of our minds, and then the outside of our lives, is to decipher to ourselves right on the spot, as we're being jarred by these emotions, their hidden, threatening language—to stand there inside our minds, *pausing*, and focus on the hidden meaning of these emotions with such passionate intensity and tenacity that the spell they're trying to cast over us weakens and breaks down like a destructive storm breaking up and passing away.

And we would be changed, powerfully free and calm for the moment. For at least this moment, these painful feelings won't be able to throw us or commandeer our thoughts or our actions.

And the decoded meaning that powers up our dark emotions is simply this: upset and disappointment with our world and the consoling magical wish for another one to appear in order to feel perfectly and everlastingly safe from all danger and threats. This is it, this is the meaning that lives in each of these emotions. Here is the algorithm of our limbic system.

But this is still not enough yet to grasp the power of this source of pain inside our brain. In order to adjust up our courage and the intensity of our gaze to get this job done well, I need to give you a feeling for time as a substance, for how our minds collect the moments of our lives into clusters.

Time isn't as abstract as we tend to think it is. It isn't really abstract at all. It's as abstract as air or gravity. And time is the habitat of awareness. Our awareness lives and moves around immersed in it, the way fish live in the sea or birds in the air.

Lights down.

Scene 14

But First I Badly Need to Give You More Proof that there are Moments Inside Our Brains, Clusters and Clusters of 'em

This notion of Time embodied, of years past but not separated from us, it was now my intention to emphasize as strongly as possible in my work.

Marcel Proust
In Search of Lost Time,
Time Regained (1927)

One Single Painful Emotion—
To See the Emotion Itself as a Thing Apart

Lights come up.

[Among other things in this scene, Consciousness enjoys the nature imagery and would like to just sit by a window and take in the view.]

We humans are remarkable animals in the way our minds collect moments into vivid clusters of experiences.

An example of this is the weather. For those of us who live some distance from the equator or the poles, there are clusters of moments in our minds for each of the different kinds of weather we've known. Year after year we take in moments drenched with the moods of the passing seasons. Through the years, each mood grows to have a vivid place in our minds. All of the different kinds of snowfalls we've witnessed are there: the brief, swirling snowfalls that lead to a dusting; or the ones that start off windless and peaceful and turn, through the hours, into slanting blizzards that mute the daylight in our homes all afternoon and go on into the night, leaving bright, sunny mornings in their wakes, heaped everywhere with sparkling drifts. And there's a collection inside of all the March winds blowing through the bare, end-of-winter landscapes we've known. And all of the warming spring times. And the hot, green Julys. And the autumns with dead leaves that whirl around in the sharp sunlight, scraping the pavement and blowing into things, or just lying everywhere in chilly rains.

These stored experiences of the world inside are so vivid because they're each saturated with so much time. We may lose almost the entire physical universe in each of our moments as they pass, but something of the moments themselves—rendered by our minds—somehow remain inside with us, stored with enough light to be seen again and again. When remembrance takes us back to them, or when we see a painting or read a description, or when the season itself returns, we reestablish contact with the rich cluster of old moments inside, falling once again under its rich spell, resonating once more with its saturated imagery.

Beside the seasons of the year stored in our minds, there are also clusters of other moments involving things we *do*: playing with toys or dolls, reading books, playing a musical instrument or baseball, riding a bike, dancing, hanging out with friends, searching online etc.

These clusters of moments also take form and accumulate inside like the moods of a season, and they stay intact and move around in our minds for as long as we live, like things in a solar system. Some people become locked in a mysterious grip of one of these activities and stay involved with it for a lifetime. It may become the inspiration for a career or a lifelong fascination. Or we may just have these experiences, enjoy them for a time, and then move on. The moments then fall away into the depths of our minds where we may return someday to recollect them or perhaps never experience them again.

It's an odd truth about the life of the mind that whenever we're in the act of experiencing something right now (which is always), we can fall back in time to different clusters of old moments—other old experiences that pull on us once again with what once happened. And if the cluster inside is large and powerful enough (our limbic system), and if we're not strong enough to resist it, it can pull us back and away from the present so fiercely, so suddenly, and hold us in such a deep spell with old feelings and secret meanings still so very real and beguiling, that we're pulled away entirely from the universe coming into view and our present moment is gone—*poof!*—before we can get to experience much of what's in it. The living moments of our lives are lost to us this way. And we can never again seize the potential—our potential—which might have come to life in them. Never.

Lights down.

Scene 15

Okay Folks, Now Here's How that Old Thing Inside Your Mind Grows and Grows and Grows!

Night and day
Under the hide of me
There's an oh such a hungry yearning
Burning inside of me.

Cole Porter
Night and Day (1932)

"I don't want realism. I want magic! Yes, yes, magic!"
Blanche Dubois

Tennessee Williams
A Streetcar Named Desire (1947)

Lights come up.

[*Among other things in this scene, Consciousness thinks about Hartman's work, how tricky, how almost impossible it is. Consciousness's attention often goes out the window to the scenes of springtime in the town. Hartman notices the straying attention.*]

Now I want to draw your attention into the heart of that concentrated collection of moments inside our minds (our limbic system), which, I'm suggesting, when it is not held in check better by our awareness, is the source of human darkness. We don't experience this collection visually, like the seasons, but instead as pure *emotion*. And we may not *see* the way it enchants us, the way we don't see the gravity pulling our bodies to Earth, or the gravity subtly pulling our fluids to the Moon, or the gravity pulling everything in our world and the whole solar system toward the Sun. Songwriters, moviemakers, writers and other artists draw their material from this old mass of moments. Every human who has ever lived senses it there and struggles with it, or the songs and the art it inspires would not be valued as they are.

This dense collection inside, like all of the other ones, is also made like a moon or a planet and pulls on our attention. But this one is much larger and more compelling than all the rest, so its pull can be even more fierce. This one is concerned with humans and with love, security and survival—with our *yearning* to be loved by the people who were important to us so that we could feel very special (and safe), and also with the *disappointment* that often followed.

(The rest of this scene we're in and of Act I will be confined to the way emotional pain develops in our minds and impacts our awareness and, consequently, our lives. The exclusive focus of this discussion on the development of our emotional pain may have the unintended effect of implying that emotional pain is *all* that's going on inside, and that we're always succumbing to it. Clearly, this is not the case. There are many lines of psychological development proceeding inside our minds, and many other experiences our awareness is having, which are relatively free of emotional pain. But I believe that how this powerful source of our emotional pain develops and the way it operates in our lives is one of the most decisive, and disturbing, of all lines of human development.)

As humans—mammals, primates—we're helpless and needy animals for at least the formative years of our lives (if not for all of them). As infants, we needed to be provided for in many physical ways: food, warmth, freedom from illness, physical contact, etc. If the particular balance we needed was off, we communicated our yearnings and our helplessness with distress, as a way to restore the balance. This distress was the only way we had as infants to communicate our needs.

Also from the start and as we grew, we had psychological needs. We yearned to be looked at and noticed. We yearned for affection, acceptance, understanding, approval, guidance, security, and love. Whether we knew it or not, we were yearning for the feeling that we were worthy and deserving enough to be loved, a kind of food for our survival. And we took all of our yearnings into our encounters with the mysterious, elusive humans who were there for us.

In childhood, each moment silently and mysteriously floods in. Each moment is alive and enchanting in some way. Some of our moments were very strongly charged with our yearning, and with the suspense and anticipation concerning when and how much love and attention the people in our presence might bestow upon us.

As children, we didn't think twice about yearning. It probably seemed that there was no difference at all between us and our yearning, that we were one with it. There was no way for us to know then that our awareness is a different substance, a different kind of electrical activity in our brain from our yearning, which from deep inside, can flare up through us and fill our awareness momentarily, taking us on a sudden magic flight to a perfect world, and then die down as though it were a primitive form of life in our brain. Our yearning feeds us with a primitive sort of direction it thinks we need in order to feel just right. And we act on our yearning instinctively. No one was there to help us notice all of this going on inside and make these distinctions.

And of course, there were many happy moments in childhood, too. Sometimes we each got even more than we dreamed of, like on birthdays, holidays, and special moments of being loved and feeling so good and safe. The glow of this satisfaction was so wonderful it set the standard for what the purest happiness could be.

But in many moments what we got was not what we yearned for, and our feeling fell short of that perfect feeling we had inklings of. We sensed something was missing: the right amount, the right timing, or exactly the right feeling—and our yearning then shaded into one of disappointment. And the disappointment that came sometimes seeped in the way nighttime seeps into day. Or sometimes it struck with sudden, painful blows of hurt, humiliation and anger, and its sting was devastating, mobilizing in our limbic mind the fight against such an imperfect world.

Yearning and *disappointment,* in all of their subtle shades, are beyond our control as children, and both can go completely unnoticed by others, even if we try to communicate them through our distress. But they were never unnoticed by us. We felt their reverberations. We may not have been fully aware of what we felt—we may not have known them to be separate from us inside our brains, and we may not have known their potential to harm us—because as children we were only slowly coming into awareness. But we could sense they were there.

Yearning for love—disappointment. Yearning for acceptance—disappointment. Yearning for affection—disappointment. Yearning—disappointment. Slight or great, occurring, when they occurred, during all of those moments at home, at school, with friends, or with ourselves, over and over.

These two feelings are joined into a single feeling in the moments in which they occur, like a molecule. A molecule of flight/fight. And like all of our moments, they fell away into our minds and were deposited together with other similar moments, like the moments inside of, say, the moods of winter. And as we grew older, all of these moments of our yearning to feel just right and our disappointment when it didn't happen, kept falling into our minds, massing together along with what was genetically given into this strange, powerful amalgam.

As the years went by, we came to realize more and more that our yearning to be loved did not rule the world of humans. Far from it. We couldn't hope to control a person we needed the way we could a crayon or a baseball. And yet we couldn't so easily decide to be done with people when we felt so uncertain, helpless, or lost in a strange and overpowering world. We were not yet aware of our own powers and believed that the love we needed was in someone else's possession. We aged, and as the pressures grew to perform and contribute, whether we became aware of it or not—usually not—we fell more and more into the grip of this growing mass of feeling inside. We grew accustomed to its presence and then we didn't think twice about it, or maybe even once.

And, insidiously, it began to shape the tones of our voices, what we said, our postures, and the clothes we chose to wear. It shaped the cars we drove, career choices, feelings about money and success, God, and life.

The pull on our awareness by the clusters of moments inside our minds concerned with something less significant like a sport or a musical instrument is like the pull of a little moon circling a planet. The moon can excite desire or tug on a sea. But the pull on us by the yearning for human love and everlasting safety, and the disappointment it can lead to, is more like the huge, silent pull of a star. It can hold us close in its orbit forever and enliven us so with the warmth of its light, or burn us with the fierceness and indifference of its power.

*   *   *

Later in life, when we encounter a situation or a person thwarting our way to fulfillment, we naturally desire a solution to the problem we're facing. We can choose to stay in the present moment if we have the strength to accept its limitations and possibilities. Or our strength can give way (as it often has for us humans throughout history) and we will lose our steady grip on our situation and go falling back into the old feeling inside our minds. And then our old yearning for a perfect solution (flight), along with the old disappointment and rejection it led to (fight), come flaring through awareness again, blending together by their strange alchemy into our feeling of anger, fear, or desperation, etc.—in other words, we cry in distress, as we did as infants.

What I'm talking about here is just the momentary strange fallback in time in each *single painful emotion.* In the throes of each feeling, the present moment is no longer something new and rich and mysterious to us. We're not even in it anymore. The moment turns, instead, into renewed contact with the pain from our past, because that's where we've fallen back to.

This mass of old experience, of old moments embedded in our minds, in the old circuits of our brains, is what I sense looming and flaring up in each mind I work with. This is where our pain arises. It's not at all from the world. And it's not us. It's *inside* with us. It's the desperate sorcery of overheated memory we harbor *inside* our very own brains.

Lights down.

Scene 16

How Far Back in Time Can Consciousness Fall in a Single Moment of Emotional Pain? Back to Our Childhoods? Back to the Time of Our Ancestors? To Medieval Times? Ancient Times? Prehistoric Times?

We have the falling sickness.

William Shakespeare
Julius Caesar (1599)

The Anatomy of a Single Painful Emotion

Lights come up.

[*Among other things in this scene, Consciousness thinks of Hartman as the anatomy teacher in Gross Emotional Anatomy class.*]

Here's a concise typical sequence, a spray of illuminating bullets, concerning what happens during the experience of a single painful emotion as our awareness falls away from the present moment back into the past:

- There we each are in the present moment.
- Limits impose themselves on us and become problems to face and try to overcome. That is, circumstances develop that impede us: traffic, other people's agendas, the weather, ill health, or constraints of time or money, etc.
- If, in the face of these limits, we have the strength to continue

to experience what the present moment is all about (Act II)—realizing what we can and cannot change, and discovering whatever possibilities there are for us—then we'll stay in the moment and handle it with a calm, accepting effort.

- If our awareness is not strong enough, it gives up control of our life in our present moment and then that mass of old moments preserved and humming away deep in our brains will take over (a more primitive way to cope) and a painful emotion urgently wishing for magic will flare, like dread, frustration, etc., to try to deal with the outer challenge we're facing.

- Falling toward something is the same as being pulled by it. So this strange old mass of feeling inside pulls on our awareness when it's too weak to deal with a challenge. Its gravity pulls on us and flares painful emotion through us. We're under its spell then and will feel like we *are* our pain. And then *we* will feel ourselves yearning for another, more perfect world, and *we* will be disappointed with the one we're in, and reject the world, and then here's what happens.

- When we're in the act of feeling impatient with a long line we're standing in, we've fallen back to old feeling and, in our primitive way, out of our disappointment, we are **rejecting** our situation and yearning for the long line to vanish.

- When we feel angry about the way someone is treating us, we've fallen into our past, and we're in the throes of **rejecting** the way that person is treating us. We're yearning for a different feeling from that person (or maybe a different person altogether than the one right there in front of us).

- And if we were to feel hatred, just think of how far back in time we've fallen, how much **rejection** we're feeling, and what we might do while we're there.

- A feeling of emotional pain is a momentary, total **rejection** of what's going on in our immediate surroundings, **rejection** of the present moment in our life. It's a **rejection**, on a small or large scale, of the only world we have to live in and work with.

- It seems like just a brief emotion passing through. You might say that these nasty feelings are important for us to have and experience. They remind us of who we are, how sane we really are, and how reasonable our needs and expectations are in a crazy, unreasonable world. But I believe these emotions are not just quiet reminders of who we are and what's reasonable to expect. They have too much force in them. They don't need to sweep through us in such gusts. They blow the world away and interfere with our relationships, our moods, our concentration, and the calm work we have to do in this moment to cope with it, let alone the possibility of experiencing the wonder of it all. And in the face of more serious events in life, these feelings can flare into horrendous turmoil and emotional illness.

- Yet we come to accept that a painful emotion is a painful emotion, and that's that. We rely on some change in the world or the movement of time to carry us away from it.

- But I have to keep pressing the case in more and more colorful ways that a painful emotion is not simply just a painful emotion. **To reiterate: I believe it marks the turning point in the life of therapy, and in life itself, when we realize *while it's flaring* that a painful emotion is a distinctly different kind of energy from our awareness and comes from a different part of our mind, a more primitive, deeper place in our brain** (our limbic system, where old threatened and frightened moments are collected from our childhood, our ancestry, and our evolutionary past). To experience a negative emotion is to undergo a kind of time travel and, because of all the havoc caused by what we're falling back into, we experience a partial or significant loss of awareness of Now.

- *Another way to understand what happens when a painful emotion flares is by thinking about color blending.* When we experience a painful emotion, like anger, for instance, it's as though we are seeing purple.

- Purple is a secondary color on the color wheel. It's a blend of two primary colors—red and blue.

- So when we're seeing purple, what we're actually experiencing is not really purple, but red and blue mixing together.

- When we're feeling painfully *envious* of someone, we're experiencing old accumulated yearning to have been more fortunate, perfectly fortunate, the way we think the person we're envying was and is, plus old accumulated disappointment over not having been fortunate enough. We're experiencing purple (envy), which is a blend of red (yearning) and blue (disappointment).
- The feeling of *fear* is saying, "I badly need something safer and more secure than this (yearning), but I'm not getting it (disappointment)."
- The feeling of *sadness* says, "I long for whatever is happening here to happen differently (yearning), but I'm not getting it (disappointment)."
- And so on down the list. Every painful emotion expresses this same blend of feeling: *"I yearn for, need, expect, or demand something, but I'm not getting it, and I'm disappointed about this."*
- **Our limbic system was designed for flight and fight, containing the fastest nerves in our bodies. Each dark emotion that flares contains an expression of flight (a fiery yearning for what could be) and one of fight (a distressing disappointment with and rejection of what's actually there).**
- And the intensity with which our painful emotions flare—that is, how far back in time we go and how primitive we become—depends on three things.

  1. The magnitude of the obstacle we're facing in the present moment
  2. How much disappointment and threatened yearning has accumulated in our life, in our ancestry, and in our genetic history (the inherited condition of our amygdalae and limbic system)
  3. The strength our awareness has to sustain the pause which helps us resist the pull back in time and holds us steady in the present moment

To see this going on in people is to witness one of the oddest things about being a human. And yet it's there all the time.

Our limbic system is certainly not a vision thing. It doesn't represent a healthy ideal that guides us, or one by which to calmly measure our progress through life. It's not concerned at all with accepting the world as it is and using our efforts to improve it. Rather, it's purely interested in needing to be safe from danger and the magic of having what it thinks it badly needs right now—Presto Changeo! And it interferes terribly with living our lives. It spoils any opportunity to experience serenity. It hampers our movement through the present like a wind overpowering a sailing ship, tearing at the sails and blowing it off course.

But the old feeling embedded in our brain is a part of our inheritance from more dangerous times. It tries to keep us safe in its own way. Perhaps anything that is alive and exposed to danger in the wilderness always wants more than it ever has—food, security, love. But its excessive influence over us and our affairs impairs our functioning and interferes with the workings of civilization. We could begin to evolve beyond its oppression by growing the necessary strength in our awareness to overpower it more effectively when we need to and have it serve us instead of the other way around.

Lights down.

Scene 17

How Many Moments of Emotional Pain Have I Collected in My Childhood, Doc? How Many Moments is this Thing in My Mind Made of? Doc, Give it to Me Straight.

It is this invisible substance of time that I have tried to isolate.

Marcel Proust,
in a 1913 interview referring
to his work, *In Search of Lost Time*

Lights come up.

[*Among other things in this scene, Consciousness would still prefer to calculate the percentage of happiness in childhood.*]

How large is this mass of old negative feeling inside? How densely packed with old painful moments are both our amygdalae, you ask? Well, there are millions of years of strong feelings about danger in the wilderness packed inside our amygdalae prior to our birth. But how many new moments of negative feelings occupy us in our childhoods? Each moment in early life of yearning to be loved, and of disappointment, can be different in duration and intensity. And they can overlap and wash into one another throughout the days of our childhood, like ocean waves on the shore. And yet, though they may be almost impossible to count as our interactions with people come and go, the moments of emotional pain do begin, and they do end. And they are counted and massed together into this huge dark force of our limbic system.

To help get a sense of the size of this mass of feeling inside, we can ask another question: what *percentage* of our waking moments throughout our childhoods did we struggle with our yearning for love and our disappointment over not being loved enough? In what percentage of our early lives did these feelings flare and put us at odds with our present moment? Was it 1 percent of the time? 10 percent? 50 percent? It may seem a ridiculous computation to attempt, but even the crudest approximation will yield a sense of the power of the mass of old moments and feeling inside every human mind.

Let's say a typical waking day in childhood was fourteen hours long, leaving ten hours for sleep. If we spent only *1 percent* of our waking day, about eight minutes, struggling with disappointed yearnings, by the time we reached eighteen, the mass of feeling and memory would be made of about *seven hundred hours*. Seven hundred hours of disappointed yearning pulling on us as we encounter this single present moment of time right now. And one percent of our childhood is probably a very modest estimate of the emotional pain each of us has struggled with. When I go to a supermarket and see children with a parent, I can witness handfuls of moments of distress and emotional pain generated in these children. Easily 1 percent of a child's day can be spent right there in the supermarket. And this may be before they even get to the cashier, where the gum and the candy are.

If *10 percent* of a childhood day, about an hour and a half, is spent struggling with yearnings to be loved and disappointment, this mass of feeling inside would be a solid *six and a half thousand hours* by adulthood, exerting an even stronger pull.

It seems a strange thing to do with moments—to turn them into something that has the shape and the pulling effect of something large, like a moon or a planet. But this is the sort of effect I keep encountering in every mind, and this kind of pull is what I find needs to be acknowledged, counteracted, and broken free of in order to feel consistently better about being alive.

Now if, in a very painful, traumatic childhood, *50 percent* or more of the time (about seven waking hours a day) is spent struggling with yearnings to be loved and disappointment over not being loved enough, this mass of feeling would be made of almost *thirty-three thousand hours (almost two million minutes)*. **Thirty-three thousand solid hours** of feeling disappointment with the world as it is and yearning for a more fulfilling one, brought to bear on our awareness as it deals with the single moment that is happening right now.

It's not unrealistic to say that most of us probably have thousands and thousands of hours, millions of small moments of emotional pain, however mild or intense, concentrated and stored in these two solid masses of feeling inside our brain (our amygdalae), their gravity reaching in every inner direction, pulling quietly all the time, then flaring and pulling harder when a more serious obstacle looms.

How powerful and influential are millions of moments of emotional pain gathered together inside our minds, flaring up, pulling, and taking over, as we try to contend with the single, challenging, present moment we're in right now? What would a million moments of playing violin sound like? Or learning to dance? Or studying mathematics or art? Or learning to know ourselves?

What experts we become at suffering from and rejecting the only world we have and yearning our hearts out for a more perfect one in order, ironically, to feel good about ourselves and our lives.

We can begin to get a sense from these calculations of how strong our awareness would have to become to resist the pull of these dense masses of feeling inside our brains. For thousands of years, civilization has never seriously taught us about this. We all become adults without knowing very well how to build the strength and freedom we'll need in our awareness in order to encounter and navigate well this most awesome and very fleeting instant we have to spend our entire lives in.

Lights down.

Scene 18

Abstract? You Think this is Abstract?
I'll Give Ya Abstract!

It's as large as life, and twice as natural.

Lewis Carroll
Through the Looking Glass (1872)

Lights come up.

[*Among other things in this scene, Consciousness watches as Hartman speaks without moving, deadpan.*]

So you think all of this is maybe a little too abstract?

Is it abstract that awareness is located inside of our minds? And that we're facing this very moment, which is like a huge, teeming ocean out there? And that time is washing in and out, always leaving these moments behind inside our minds? Is this abstract? Mystical, spiritual, cosmic, or real, maybe, but not abstract.

And is it so abstract that as children we yearn for one kind of love or another? And that our yearnings are for a perfect love and safety, and that they mostly shade into disappointment to one degree or another because moments of perfect love are so infrequent and intermittent?

And is it so abstract to think that these moments of yearning, which turn into disappointment, collect and grow inside our minds like pearls in oysters, like gigantic pearls, and become pure, solid masses of memory that can pull on us with a terrific force? The past may be gone, but it hasn't separated from us. It's right there inside. Is this so abstract?

And is it abstract to think that the present moment we're facing right now can also feel baffling, mystifying, and challenging to our strength?

71

And that when we can't stay in this moment and deal with what's in it, we fall back into that past inside our minds, where old, magical hope is waiting, because life is just too damned hard to accept *as it is*? And that when we fall back, we find no magic there, either—just the old yearning for magic, and disappointment? So what we get is a nasty blend of these two, and we feel one or more of those painful emotions on the grand list of all painful emotions. Whoosh … anger comes. And whoosh … hopelessness comes. Is this really so abstract? Ironic, maybe.

A negative painful emotion is an unbelievably sudden fallback in time, like falling out of a tree. And what we're left with is a strong nasty feeling, which basically says "No!" Then we have to climb our way back up into the present moment again. What's so abstract about this?

I'm trying to convey a sense of the gravitational pull this thing has inside our brain, the powerful old one-two in every painful emotion, and, most importantly, the weakness in our awareness to resist it. I'm providing the exact address of the problem in human self-esteem, the evolutionary dilemma in our brains, which we can solve when our awareness grows to be so strong that it tips the balance of power in its favor. I'm making it all as concrete as I can, bricks and shingles, as concrete as the home we once lived in, where, apart from what our ancestors contributed, all of our emotional pain happened once upon a time.

Still not quite concrete enough? Okay, here's some more concrete for you…

Lights down.

Scene 19

Yes, That Old Thing Inside Our Minds is Very Large and Very Dark!

No light, but rather darkness visible

John Milton
Paradise Lost (1665)

Lights come up.

[*Among other things in this scene, Consciousness thinks about Hartman, the astronomer.*]

In deep space between the stars and at the heart of every galaxy, there exists a kind of object that resembles the strange old mass of feeling inside our minds. It's a kind of star; really the remains of a star. It no longer shines, but it continues to exist, and its pull on its surroundings is tremendous.

Stars are like humans. They're born, live their lives, and die. As far as its fate goes, each star starts off with two kinds of matter. One kind burns to create light; the other is heavier, denser, doesn't burn and creates no light. What marks the end of a star's light-giving days is the depletion of the matter producing light. When this moment comes, a huge explosion of luminous gases occurs, called a supernova, as the remaining matter undergoes a sudden, dramatic, gravitational collapse into itself. And if the star is about the size of the Sun, which could hold about a million Earths, it collapses, in the span of moments, into a super-dense, lightless mass no more than about ten miles in diameter, and it's called a neutron star. The amount of matter in *one pinhead* of this thing has been calculated to weigh *one million tons*. The gravitational pull from a mass like this is so great that a baby weighing nine pounds on Earth would weigh *90 billion pounds* on a neutron star. And if the star that dies is huge enough to begin with, the mass that collapses into itself after the light is gone is so dense and can pull so powerfully that even nearby light streaming by gets pulled into it and vanishes. Then it's called a black hole.

The dense things inside our brain—our amygdalae—from where painful emotions flare up resemble neutron stars, or black holes. But they're not made of neutrons, because our minds are filled with time. Rather, they're made of moments, all of the moments of yearning (flight) for the most perfect feeling of safety and love, and all of the disappointment (fight) over not receiving it, compressed into strangely blended and concentrated masses of feeling that produce every kind of painful emotion.

Under stress, and when we're not feeling strong and steady, we can lose our hold on the present moment and fall back into old childhood ways. And we don't go freely back into our past. We fall. Awareness falls away, because it's not strong enough to resist how powerfully our deep old need for magical relief pulls on the insides of our minds. And just like neutron stars or black holes, these things inside our minds are the remains of what once was. No new light comes from them. All they have left are their masses and their strong pull.

These remains know nothing about dealing with Now. They're made purely out of past time; they can't know about Now. They are then, purely then, hulking there inside our minds. They don't care about limitations and realistic possibilities. In their primitive efforts to protect us and keep us safe and secure, and help us cope with reality, all they seem to do is pull with their concentration of old moments and old feelings, casting powerful worried, frightened, angry, etc. spells over us.

Positive thinking alone doesn't have a chance of pulling us out of these spells. It can only lift us up for a little while, like a helium balloon.

To break these old spells we have to stare down our limbic system with a very steady, unshakeable gaze. We have to see our amygdalae for what they are: powerful, dense masses of old, disappointed yearning/worry/fear/anger, etc., that are like living creatures, neurologically designed to forever believe that what could have been and what could be is more important than what is. To break the dark and distorted spells they cast, we have to hold still and resist their pull using the most potent realizations—realizations that are like powerful wings...

Lights down.

Scene 20

And the Darn Thing Seems So Alive and So Awfully Enchanting, Doesn't it?

In the center of the chair was an enormous Head, without body to support it or any arms or legs whatever. There was no hair upon this head, but it had eyes and nose and mouth, and was bigger than the head of the biggest giant.

L. Frank Baum
The Wonderful Wizard of Oz (1900)

Breaking a Single Painful Emotion Down into its Four Enchanting Illusions

Lights come up.

[*Among other things in this scene, Consciousness thinks about Hartman, the illusion slayer.*]

We succumb to a strange enchantment as we experience a single painful emotion. Right there, when we're being called upon by the universe to deal with the moment we're in and it isn't complying with our wishes, we get jarred from the inside of our minds by a strong reaction, i.e., the negative emotion. This is where our troubles are in life, and this is where we break through them. If we could get a hold of ourselves in a new way during the very experience of this reaction, *as it's happening*, we might just see something in the world we usually overlook. And then we might make a slightly different choice of words or actions, and have different effects on people and circumstances, and this could change the course of our lives. And it might change the course of the way things go in the whole world, too.

When we flare with annoyance at some incompetence we witness and may be a victim of; when we rattle with anxiety or fear over the possibility of something terrible happening; when we plunge into a sad, irritable mood and we're not even sure why—it *feels* like the emotion just overcomes us. It feels like we've had no choice in the matter. It flares up from an uneasy place in our brain, and suddenly we're in the grip of it. It feels like a reflex—it happens so fast.

If we could slow down our awareness enough and hold it very steady while the emotion is flaring, we could witness potent and bewitching illusions coming at us from what's in that chair deep inside our minds (our limbic system). And when you can calmly realize that something you once believed was so true turns out to be just an illusion, it's the way to break the most powerful of spells.

There are *four of these illusions we experience simultaneously*, four ways we are seduced and fooled as we succumb to a single painful feeling:

Illusion #1 is that something out there in the world is causing our upset and should be gone, replaced immediately with a better set of circumstances. Think of what happens at the very surface of our experience of feeling angry or worried. At the surface of the feeling, we're in the process of rejecting something going on in the world that's displeasing to us. And the feeling is usually so engulfing that we tend to reject almost the whole situation out there. In the throes of a painful emotion, we utter a big "No!" to the world.

Illusion #2 has to do with the way the two components (the disappointment with what's happening and the yearning for something better) become disguised as they blend by their strange alchemy into the raw experience of our negative feeling. As I described in scene 16, any painful emotion is actually the blending of two feelings, just as purple is actually a blend of blue and red. *Disappointment* with the situation (blue), and *yearning* for another one (red), mix together in different intensities (depending upon the degree to which we're being thwarted by the world, our childhood and ancestral pain, and the strength of our awareness) and turn into all the different shades of our negative feelings, all the different shades of purple.

Illusion #3 is that the "voice" in the feeling of pain is really our voice. When any feeling of pain flares suddenly and strongly, it carries a kind of "voice" with it, containing its own logic, sent from that old system in our brain. We become one with our pain as it flares and overpowers us, and we fall under the illusion that this "voice" is *our* voice, that *we* are the one rejecting the situation in the world, that *we* are the one yearning another world, similar to the way a cult member succumbs to the charisma of the cult leader and adopts the beliefs conveyed through the leader's haunting voice. But this voice is not the voice of our awareness; it's actually separate from us anatomically inside our brain, yet its pull flares completely through us like gravity. You can tell that a painful emotion is not *us* because when it subsides, *we* are still there but *it* is gone.

This "voice" in our painful emotions comes speaking to us through the distance of years that have been collected deep in our minds. It flares up and doesn't make a sound, yet it resounds in our minds. And it says this, loud and clear:

I can't stand this.

I want to feel *that* way instead of this.

I need *that* instead of this.

I can't stand what you told me.

I wish you had said *that* instead of this.

I want *that* to be happening instead of this.

I want it to be *that* moment instead of now.

I need *that* universe instead of this.

I can't stand this.

The "voice" isn't expressing a simple preference for things to be another way, which would be healthier and lead to a plan and real efforts to achieve it. What happens when we're weak and we fall under the spell of this "voice" is that we become controlled by the painful sorcery in it. It demands another reality to appear without us having to make any effort at all. No effort, just magic, and it says: "I can't stand you" … "That person's an idiot" … "That organization is all screwed up" … "The world sucks" …

This "voice" in our negative feeling can pull very hard on us at times, especially when we're unusually stressed and weak, just as we feel physical gravity more sharply when we fall suddenly from a height.

But even when we're not facing something in the present moment that's challenging and stressful, this "voice" is there quietly permeating our minds, "speaking" and pulling, silently and ceaselessly, like the pull of the Earth when we're just standing on the ground. Before we learn about our minds, and even when we do, we may not even be aware that it's pulling when it is and feel as though there's no pull at all.

And the 4th illusion we experience when a negative emotion flares up is that the "voice" in it is full of knowledge, truth and wisdom. During the moments when a painful emotion is flaring through us, we're believing that it's a great and powerful leader, or a god, who knows exactly what happiness is and how to guide us to it. And as the feeling flares, like annoyance or dread, we submit, in a flash of old innocence, to the truth we believe is in it. "Yes," we say. "What's going on <u>is</u> unacceptable. It shouldn't be going on. Something else should. Yes." We flame or shudder in submission to this "voice" speaking inside us like some ancient, forbidding deity.

*   *   *

A raw feeling flares.

Under the spell cast by the flaring of this feeling *inside* our mind, we are made to believe that the *outside* world is the cause of our unhappiness, insecurity and pain.

We don't pause to think that this feeling is a strange blend of disappointment and yearning for magic.

And we also don't believe that the "voice" casting the spell is not us, but rather the "voice" of concentrated, old feeling coming at us from another part of our mind, another part of our brain.

And we surrender to this past of ours, to our limbic system, as if it were a cult leader, or a god, who has the ultimate anguished wisdom about life.

All of this in one single painful emotion.

Lights down.

Scene 21

And Yes, it Speaks with a Voice, a Voice that Grips All of You and Me and Pulls so Strong and Fast Before We Can Even Think, Just Like Gravity When We Fall. Please, Somebody!

As Dorothy gazed upon this in wonder and fear the eyes turned slowly and looked at her sharply and steadily. Then the mouth moved, and Dorothy heard a voice say: 'I am Oz, the Great and Terrible.'

L. Frank Baum
The Wonderful Wizard of Oz (1900)

Appreciating More Deeply the Way a Single Painful Emotion has the Same Effect as a Voice Bewitching Us to Believe the Wrong and Painful Thing

Lights come up.

[*Among other things in this scene, Consciousness thinks about listening to all of the hope in a doll's voice.*]

A negative emotion happens so very fast. It flares right through us. Set off by an obstacle of some kind we encounter in the world right now, it can linger and gnaw, or pass away quickly:

Apprehensive about a physical symptom that's not going away …
Frustrated with a defiant child …

Weary of rainy weather day after day ...

Afraid while waiting for a spouse or a child expected a long time ago and still not home ...

Exasperated by traffic ...

Disgusted when someone seems to be refusing to understand ...

Worried about a political event...

A negative emotion can be a very small event inside that no one else sees. A single negative emotion is the smallest unit of emotional pain we feel. And just look at it. Doesn't it seem like just a part of the human condition, like witnessing an act of nature, like feeling a raindrop hit? Although negative emotions may be small and brief, one big problem with them is that they happen on their own and with such force, and without awareness playing any active part in them. They flare up from inside our minds and come from a source inside that's separate from our own will. They are responses to stress. And they act like solutions to problems we're having, but they don't solve anything. They don't do any real work. They just hamper us. And they are what can accumulate and intensify, like raindrops, into terrible storms of illness: anxiety, panic, and depression.

*   *   *

And so our painful emotions come rushing through our minds, flaring into our lives.

It's worth focusing a little more on the idea that a dark emotion has the quality of a voice. We humans have an innate ability to relate to, and understand, the character of other beings and things in the cosmos, like galaxies, microorganisms, pets, fellow humans, moments then and now, etc. We naturally impart that sense of cohesion to things we feel in ourselves so we can relate to them. And we also have an ability to change how we relate to them, and how we feel about them, once we've understood them. Relating to our limbic system as though it were a kind of being with a voice and a character, even though this is an illusion, may be a way to help us change our relationship with it and prevent ourselves from falling so blindly into its grip.

And one powerful counterintuitive thing we could understand and "see" at the very heart of any negative emotion is hope, a trace of our oldest hope, the hope that still lives in our old yearning deep inside to be safe from danger and to be loved. In some fast unconscious way, as we succumb to the spell of a painful emotion, we're longing momentarily for some redeeming hope our limbic system is badly needing. This is why we get so emotional and negative: we're actually hoping deep down—grasping urgently with the force of our emotion—for something much better the only way we know how to in that moment.

In the flash of a single emotion, our awareness makes such a poignant painful journey, surrendering and falling back into our past, drawn to that old primitive sweet hope we're "hearing" somewhere in the strange, swirling "voice" of the distressing emotion flaring through us. This is our amygdalae "speaking" to us.

In our surrender to these feelings, we give up everything special about us in the present moment. We give up our own special voice and the part *we* can play in our life, and we become just another expression of the "voice" of this old feeling inside. We put ourselves and our world under huge pressure. We try to become the arms and legs of this "voice," to do its fantastic bidding and make its magic happen. But it's not the magic of the wonder we can feel under the night sky, or the magic in an act of kindness, or the magic of all the hard work and caring that keep breaking out in our society when calamities occur. No, this is a deadlier kind of magic, a magic which needs a part of the universe, or maybe even the whole thing, to be replaced quickly, dramatically, and effortlessly.

*   *   *

But after all, this "voice" is just an old "voice" made of old moments. There's no more new light in it to guide us into the unknown, only an old pull on our spirit, longing for magic and knowing no bounds, way out of touch with any actual threats in our surroundings. The "voice" of emotional pain is not like our awareness. It can't make any contact with the present moment. It's like a powerful old enchanting echo that *feels* alive.

The actual life of these moments has passed away. It's like a doll's voice. It wants fulfillment so badly, but doubts it will ever come. Its call is nothing but what it has always done. It doesn't know fulfillment. It doesn't care that way. It's a thing that just goes on calling and echoing inside, straining powerfully in its hope and despair from the long ago inside our brain.

*   *   *

And what this old system inside our mind/brain with its "voice" will never know is that the dream of life *has* come true and it's continually coming true. It's very mysterious and imperfect, but it's fully realized and miraculous nevertheless—and it's right here all around us: it is the actual universe, teeming with presence and light and mystery and all of the enormous real potential we could ever dream of fulfilling. And it has the final word. But our limbic system with those dark stars of our amygdalae will never know this. Only *we* might; only our awareness might know.

We all emerge into adulthood still so vulnerable, still believing so much in the remains of the old starlight inside.

Lights down.

Scene 22

It's a Regular Perpetual Motion Machine! It Just Wants What it Wants When it Wants it, and Forever and Ever. Now, Isn't that Asking for Just a Little Too Much?

Through Me Come Into the City Full of Pain
Through Me Come Into Endless Suffering
I Go On Forever

> Dante Alighieri,
> from the inscription at
> the entrance to Hell
> *Cantos from Dante's Inferno* (2000)

The Way a Painful Emotion Yearns for Forevermore While Consciousness is Busy Trying to Deal with Each Moment and Let It Go

Lights come up.

[Among other things in this scene, Consciousness notices how much Hartman seems to enjoy trying to shock the hell out of his audience with metaphors.]

Our negative feelings are like momentary hypnotic spells cast by an inner "voice" sweeping quickly through us in reaction to circumstances we don't like, attempting to magically freeze and reject all of the action out there.

There's one more striking feature to notice about that system of old feeling inside our brain: **it wants what it wants to last forever**. The perfect arrangement, forever. The perfect response from someone, from everyone, forever. Perfection and bliss, forever and ever.

Think of the logic permeating any negative feeling like regret, gloom or insecurity. *Inside the very experience of the feeling* you can sense the wish for "forevermore." It's a wish for something to stop happening forevermore, and for something to start happening and last forevermore.

This old source of emotions inside our minds can act this way because it really isn't alive at all the way our awareness is alive. It fools us. We get hypnotized by it because of how many old moments it contains and the intensity and power it has in its "voice." We get enticed momentarily, unconsciously, into believing what these emotions are "saying" to us: that we could be fulfilled forever *if only what just happened had happened differently.*

Our limbic system, with its amygdalae, is a kind of perpetual motion machine. Like the awesome, ravenous gravity of dead stars, it's forever pulling on what's around it. It pulls on the awareness inside our minds, dreaming and despairing perpetually, saying, "Not enough, never enough," for as long as we live.

The present moment, with a fresh universe flooding into it, is not the concern of this perpetual motion machine inside our minds. All that concerns it when it's flaring is its perpetual yearning to be loved and taken care of, and its perpetual disappointment that there's not enough. Never ever enough. It doesn't care at all about details, or the superhuman efforts involved, or the impossibility of the fulfillment of its dream. It doesn't care that its yearning entails an immediate, magical redesign of the universe. It doesn't care that our awareness is burdened with its fulfillment. It doesn't care that, in our weakness, we take personally everything that is said and done around us. It's actually just fine with this because only then will we be troubled enough about every disappointing thing in the world to try to work the magic of turning it all into what this thing inside perpetually needs. This old mass of feeling inside doesn't even know it's not in touch with what's going on out there. All it does is yearn and need, expect and demand, and feel disappointment. It seems to think that the only way to achieve self-preservation is in a perfect world, which is never there. So it goes on yearning and is disappointed perpetually.

Perpetual motion machines don't do anything other than what they do perpetually. Any outer fulfillment will not slow down or change this thing in our minds. Its motion—its pull—is perpetual, despite fulfillment, conquests, riches, or success of any kind. This is why people who are so astonishingly successful in so many ways can be so unhappy. Our limbic system rapidly becomes indifferent to any change in our circumstances and quickly reverts to the state where there's no limit to what it yearns for. It just stays, more or less, in its motion of pulling on awareness with its hope for another world and its disappointment about this one. It is its own illusory realm of forever, needing infinite and eternal love and security in the perpetual motion of its pained yearning. There's nothing more to it but what it perpetually keeps doing. And it will always be inside with us in its perpetual motion.

But the truth about life is that there is no forever in the heart of any passing moment. All there is in the present moment, besides the whole universe, is impermanence. Any guarantee of permanence while we're alive is an illusion. Time keeps proving everything is in constant motion. If we're going to live effectively and more serenely in *this* moment, the only living moment we will ever have, our awareness has to become strong enough to accept—*we* have to become strong enough to accept—that it is what it is, that it is loaded with potential, and that it won't last.

*   *   *

So there's a machine made of old time inside our human mind, inside our brain, called our limbic system. It has primitive hope and despair. It has strange powers to pull on our awareness and take us over in the present moment when we're at our limit and we need more hope. Its an old weakness in humans. And so we give way to it, it pulls, and we feel more pain than hope.

We call this the human condition.

In every painful emotion, we fall, traveling back through the time inside our minds. In every single feeling of pain, we have surrendered. We have fallen far away from Now to dream an old dream again, a very very olde dream for a perfect love, a perfect world.

In one painful feeling after another, we each fall under the mighty spell of our past. One painful feeling after another. Disappointed and yearning. Again and again. Again and again. This *could* go on for a lifetime. It *could* last forever ... *could* last forever ... *could* last forever ...

Lights down.

Scene 23

Yes, I Know There's Weakness in You. I'm Your Therapist. You Can't Fool Me. You Know How I Know There's Weakness in You? Here's How I Know There's Weakness in You.

The greatest weakness of all weaknesses
Is to fear too much to appear weak.

Jacques Benigne Bossuet,
French churchman and orator
Statecraft Drawn from the Holy Scriptures (1709)

Lights come up.

[*Among other things in this scene, Consciousness thinks about Hartman's dark humor, and about stage fright, and how the springtime sunlight outside is so bright that it makes the office look dark.*]

When we fall back into old dark feeling (when we succumb to our over-heated limbic system) we diminish ourselves. We disappear. We turn back into our old yearning for something better and our old disappointment with whatever we have now. We reduce ourselves to these two feelings that keep blending and flaring up into guilt, futility, or any other painful feeling. We become creatures of the past, drawn back by the pull of the cold dead stars of our amygdalae in our brains where there's no more new light for our awareness, just the deadly pull back. We lose our humanity, and we become rejecting. We become disgruntled. We get disgusted. We throw things and break things. We become abusive in our pain. We yell and scream. We abduct children and abuse them. We discriminate. We vandalize. We rob. We rape. And we murder. And we're impatient, too. With our kids and our spouse, and with strangers in public. And we're passive-aggressive. We argue. We have road rage. We drive too fast and kill people by accident. We kill ourselves by accident. We commit suicide. And from our overpowering yearning for something better, we fall into addictions to alcohol, cocaine, heroin, pornography, gambling, eating, etc.

And when all we become is an old painful feeling, we can be greedy and inconsiderate. We can push and shove. And we can have very bad table manners. And we never seem to have enough money. We cheat, too. We commit white-collar crime. We pollute the world. We backbite. We can be petty, nasty neighbors, and we can be vengeful, jealous, and bitter. We can be racist and sexist and xenophobic. We can let our limbic system commit genocide and ethnic cleansing, not to mention other atrocities. Do you remember the Holocaust? Armenia? Rwanda? The Soviet Man-made famine? Bangladesh? The Greek Genocide? Cambodia? Bosnia? Darfur? Tibet? The American Indians? Et cetera. Et cetera. Et cetera.

And we can become afraid and insecure. We have affairs. We betray. We break our husband's heart, and we break our wife's heart. We can become obsessed with our image and our need to impress people. And we can be fooled. We let ourselves get pulled into cults. And one of the worst things of all is that we get stage fright. We can't bring out the best in ourselves and show 'em what we've got. We don't revolt when our lives really depend upon it. Sometimes we need to start a regular uprising, but we stand there, freeze in the headlights and get run over. We can be very passive and complacent. We can be miserable. And we can worry. Oh, can we worry. We can lose all perspective and not be able to know what really matters.

We have the potential for our awareness to become more fully evolved and **be** in the present moment, but we haven't realized it yet. Instead, we keep falling back into the nervous past deep inside our minds, pulled back by our limbic system. We turn back into the two old, dead-end feelings— our yearning to be loved perfectly, and our disappointment over not being loved perfectly enough. In other words, we experience painful emotions over and over and over, and we let them ravage us.

This is how I know there's weakness in us. This is how I know.

Curtain.

ACT II

Breaking Free of Painful Emotions and Being in the Present Moment, and I Mean Being in the Present Moment

Curtain Rises

Change' is the nursery of musicke, joy, life and eternity.

John Donne (1572–1631)
Elegy III, Change
The Complete Poetry and
Selected Prose of John Donne (1994)

I know of no more encouraging fact than the unquestionable ability of man to elevate his life by a conscious endeavor. It is something to be able to paint a particular picture, or to carve a statue, and so to make a few objects beautiful; but it is far more glorious to carve and paint the very atmosphere and medium through which we look, which morally we can do. To affect the quality of the day, that is the highest of arts.

God himself culminates in the present moment, and will never be more divine in the lapse of all the ages. And we are enabled to apprehend at all what is sublime and noble only by the perpetual instilling and drenching of the reality that surrounds us.

Henry David Thoreau
Walden (1854)

Scene 24

And Now for the Star of Our Show ... From the Great Stage ... Here's Consciousness! (Cheers and Applause)

Once upon a time, during one of the smallest fractions of a second imaginable after the Big Bang cataclysm, the entire universe visible today ... was compressed to a size even smaller than the point of a needle.

Neil McAleer
The Cosmic Mind-Boggling Book (1982)

It is through that which is most incommunicably personal in us that we make contact with the universal.

Pierre Teilhard de Chardin
How I Believe (1969)

Lights come up.

[Among other things in this scene, Consciousness hears what Hartman is saying but as part of the background of the springtime scene filling the office windows. The afternoon sunlight is streaming down into the office now at a sharper angle, getting caught sometimes in Hartman's eyeglasses as he speaks and moves in his chair.]

The human body is engaged in all sorts of actions all the time. Lungs and hearts are forcing air and blood to flow. Kidneys and livers are filtering.

Muscles are contracting. Limbs are bending. Organs are busy breaking down molecules and building them up. And awareness is seeing.

Small and luminous, our awareness hovers alone and unsteady for a lifetime in the vast space of our minds, trying to see all it can, sifting ceaselessly through the images and perceptions passing through it, except perhaps in sleep or death, although maybe then, too.

And our awareness seems so strangely given to us. It's powered by something unseen, and we depend on it in such a primitive way that we take it for granted. We tend to rely on it the way we rely on our livers. We assume it's in a finished state and it knows how to handle everything that comes its way, just like our livers. It'll do what it has to do when it has to do it.

But at some point in each of our lives, our minds will likely clash in a big way with what seems to be an implacable world. We'll be called upon to examine ourselves, to look inside, and to examine, if we can, what does the looking. We'll realize at some point that there are weaknesses in our awareness, blind spots and distortions. Our awareness is not at all finished becoming what it could be. It could use some work. None of the important people we depended upon to shape and temper us did the job as well as it needed to be done. We'll realize as grownups that it falls largely on each of us alone to find out how to finish the job. Or we'll choose not to finish it, and live with a gnawing sense of unfulfilled potential.

*   *   *

Looking at it, our awareness, hovering somewhere just behind our eyes, seems like such a small shred inside our minds. But its seeming minuteness gives way to a teeming realm. It's as deceptive a realm as that pinpoint which came into being in the instant after the start of the Big Bang containing the entire contents of our universe. As far as humanity is concerned, our awareness is like a living echo of that pinpoint; it's still exploding into our own little universe called civilization, and into the elusive, quantum realms of our personal lives.

It's strange to be aware and to be living life inside of a mind. *Seeing* is also a strange thing to be doing: always looking inside and outside, trying to see so deeply and so far beyond, and swept so by one feeling after another.

Awareness seems to be such an excitable, tenuous, elusive thing that it's hard to examine. It's hard even to keep it in focus and get a good look at it. It seems to be there only by virtue of what's passing through it, like trying to look at the substance of a mirror apart from what it's reflecting. Or it's like trying to see the light filling a room. We don't quite see the light itself; we only see what's being lit up by it.

Somehow or other, awareness is continually materializing inside our minds, experiencing a tantalizing hint of the universe which seems to coalesce for us into a present moment, and which, like awareness, is also continually materializing, but on a grand scale, and holding steady like a frame or a portal.

And whatever our awareness is exposed to in the world right now passes through it and enters the deeper, fertile space of our minds. First it becomes our recent past, but over time it becomes our deep and distant past. We can recall what we've stored away, or not. Our brain submits to our awareness, but can also overpower it, as in the case of our limbic system, which only seeks to protects us from what it perceives as danger. Our awareness shares with the deeper realms of our brain a feeling about life and about all of those moments passing through. The bond with our own mind is the first and the last bond we each have in life. It's like a human relationship, but it's even more elemental than loving someone, stronger than the most primitive dependency, and deeper than the relationships we have with other parts of our body. We can interact with and know what's inside our own mind. We can influence it in ways we never can with anything or anyone else. We never leave our own mind until we die, and we may not then, either.

And there's another strikingly simple but fateful thing about our awareness: only it can see certain things inside. Maybe someday, some magnetic imaging device will be able to detect the traces of a feeling of bafflement, say, and tell it apart from a feeling of awe. But right now, the only entity in this universe that can make this distinction is human awareness. None of what we see, inside or outside, can ever be verified by anyone with any more certainty than by our own awareness. And what we see there, we see alone, in silence. And in our acts of seeing, we can be completely invisible to the rest of humanity. Even God, for those who believe, leaves us alone in our seeing; seeing is what we do in the pure freedom of our will. It becomes entirely up to us to see and to name whatever is there.

Our awareness lives its every moment under these rather strange conditions, which, among others, will have to be taken into account in any transformation of it.

And finally, what resides in awareness is our potential, our sense of what we could become, our inner future not yet realized. It's our potential for well-being, for finding love, and finding work we love to do and maybe achieving mastery in it, and through it all to perhaps have a large and good influence on many people. And it's our potential to withstand our calamities with poise and grace, and to make all of the efforts our lives call for. Our sense of our potential is one of our most highly prized possessions. And our awareness does the work to realize this potential, when it does.

But we need to ask ourselves a question about this sense of our potential: does the way we see and yearn for it engage us enough in the hard, real work we need to do to realize it? Or is this yearning infused by such a wish for magic that it leads us, instead, to keep waiting for some kind of magician to appear?

Most of the time we encounter the spurs to our transformation by accident. We don't usually stop by anything we see long enough to see it deeply, whether it's inside our minds or out in the world. We tend to move quickly from one thing to the next, urged on by pressures, usually staying close to what's splashing against our retinas or vibrating our eardrums. Only in rare moments do we slow down and seriously look inside ourselves to generate realizations large enough to change us forever. Sometimes a deep, lasting change is set off when our circumstances in life change suddenly, like when a child leaves home, a career comes to an end, or a spectacular or tragic thing happens.

But maybe we can learn to transform ourselves more deliberately, without the catalyst of an upheaval, and free our awareness with a method, so that we could reach with it more deeply and calmly into the known and the immense unknown in this very moment? There's no doubt in any of us that somewhere in this moment, somewhere inside our awareness in this very moment, our potential is waiting for us, waiting like great works of art cocooned inside of unopened tubes of paint.

Lights down.

Two Obstacles to Believing in the Possibility of Changing Ourselves

Scene 25

Obstacle One: Living in this World of Humans that is (Bite My Tongue) Without the Priority to Have a Healthy Mind

His old impulses have been with him for millions of years, his new ones only a few thousand at the most—and there is no hope of quickly shrugging off the accumulated genetic legacy of his whole evolutionary past. He would be a far less worried and more fulfilled animal if only he would face up to this fact.

Desmond Morris
The Naked Ape (1967)

Lights come up.

[*Among other things in this scene, Consciousness watches with dismay as Hartman diagnoses a grim state of affairs in the human condition.*]

It doesn't seem to be easy for any of us to change, to be able to create that extended pause inside that improves our quality of life and helps us handle our moments.

And our culture isn't really endorsing this kind of work. It's tolerating the work, maybe. But it's not telling us emphatically that it's very important to have a healthy mind, that it ought to be the highest priority in life. And it's not showing us how to achieve it.

How many healthy minds do you see out there? I don't mean minds of high intelligence or unusual talent, and I don't mean appearances.

Look around. Is the priority being taught in schools? Do you find the priority of a healthy mind in the world of business, in medical practices, law firms, in the courts? Is it displayed in the halls of Congress? In houses of worship? Is it coming from the news media? Is it on the internet? Is it in marriages and families?

Maybe our culture, in all it does and offers, expresses some sort of positive intention about the concept of a healthy mind. But it's barely implied most of the time, so far between the lines, that it seems not to be there at all. No sure method is offered in childhood or adulthood.

Culture stands next to us and says, "Find it if you can. Find it your own way. There are self-improvement books all over the place, and treatment programs and therapy methods to beat the band. You take it from here, pal. I've got all of these other things to do. I wish you well. Good luck." And in its most caring moments, our culture puts its arm on our shoulder, pointing up to the idea of having a strong and healthy mind, as though it were a star twinkling in the sky, and says, "Yes, it is a good idea, a very good idea for you to reach for that. But I don't really know how you get there. You need to figure that out on your own. I know you can do it."

So it's pretty clear that our culture is just not seriously interested enough yet in making it a high priority for its citizens to have healthy minds. But what could be more important? It ought to be as basic to our lives as it is to wear clothing, use language, or add a column of numbers. With all of these messes that depression and anxiety are leading to out there, not to mention crime, genocide and war, a method for gaining the self-knowledge to steady ourselves ought to be right at hand, and it ought to work as effectively as an umbrella. From an early age, we each ought to be trained to understand our own emotional pain—to understand it deeply, and to handle ourselves in whatever fleeting moment we're in, the way we were trained to walk, read, and write. But no, the priority is just not out there yet. Only the merest implied hints.

Is psychological health such a revolutionary new idea that it takes getting used to? Or is it just an idea that's always been extremely elusive and hard to think much about? And—bite my tongue again—does having a healthy mind matter, anyway? Can't we make a living without one? Can't we invent all kinds of neat gadgets, build bridges and skyscrapers, do so many good things, and create stunningly beautiful works of art without having a healthy mind or thinking much about having one?

Or is psychological health actually already there in essence, without our knowing it, making everything work when it does work? Perhaps the workings of a healthy mind have remained hidden from us, and we've benefited from them by accident and taken them for granted. It may be like solar energy, which we still use in such a primitive way (as crude oil) without quite knowing yet how to harness it more directly.

Right now, it all seems to be up to practitioners like me and all of the willing participants in this strange process to get the job done with what truths we can find here together. Because civilization has a dreadful logic driving its history, haunting its functioning and threatening its survival, a logic emanating from a dominant limbic system, of whipping up large numbers of people, under the spell of their negative emotions, to make rapid, bloody changes in the world. Learning how to quell our limbic system, when we need to, by working new strength into conscious thought alone, without resorting to any other action, is to redefine our very concept of 'the human enemy' and maybe, for the sake of our survival, to help end our species' old tendency to annihilate one another. So the idea of cultivating the healthiest mind possible needs to be the supreme priority in this office. Maybe from here, and other settings like it, the priority of emotional health will keep igniting and take a high place someday in the worldwide mind of civilization. And then everything will change.

Lights down.

Scene 26

Obstacle Two: The Strangeness of Using One Little Tiny Part of Your Mind Against Another Exceedingly Huge Part, and the End of Something When You Do. It's Biblical! It's an Epic Struggle You'll Never Forget!

And to make an end is to make a beginning.
The end is where we start from.

T. S. Eliot
Four Quartets (1943)

Lights come up.

[Among other things in this scene, Consciousness wonders about the prospects of a biblical struggle.]

Obstacle one—our culture "saying" it's not such a high priority to have a healthy mind—leads to complex obstacle two—that strange feeling, when we take the time to notice it, of having a mind at all, of living inside of one, and then the still stranger activity of having an emotional breakthrough and changing the way our mind works.

Whenever we each stop and quietly regard it, our mind seems like a strange, shadowy medium with its endless inner space, its profusion of glowing images, and all the sorcery that goes on in there all day. It's also strange to have awareness and experience a world outside and be able to freely choose how we deal with it. It never really stops being strange to think about having a mind and being inside of one. It only seems to get stranger.

To make a lasting change in your life so you can count on feeling steady, comfortable and alive to your surroundings, then you have to change the way the *inside* of your mind works, no matter how strange it is to be in there.

Change means something comes to an end, and something new begins.

What comes to an end is not our frustrated old need for more love and security (limbic system), which can pull so hard from deep inside our brain, because that's made of time we've already experienced and stored away. It is what it is, and it can't be changed. Rather, what I believe comes to an end is our *relationship with it, the way we keep succumbing* to its anguished pull. Ending, changing an old relationship such as this one inside our brain will not be easy.

What I believe becomes necessary to succeed is the creation of a pause, to be able to pause and hold our awareness very still while an onslaught of emotion is getting underway, rising from the limbic system. The challenge is to be able to feel the stillness and the turmoil at the same time. The effort to pause is an act of will; the emotion welling up is not. It is the limbic mind flaring its emotion in response to some danger it senses, which this system so often perceives to be present when no real danger is actually there. And so if you maintain this pause, keeping a strong boundary around it, it will provoke your limbic system to redouble its efforts and test your resolve to keep pausing. Learning to protect and strengthen this pause is what I see in my work with people as the turning point in life. It can become invincible with practice.

Your limbic system will sound its alarm, needing your awareness to become alarmed, too. It is threatened by what it's sensing outside. It's needing more than it's getting. And it needs to get you to protest, to fight, to blast the world, to flee into magical thinking because the world is not being better than it is. You're limbic mind needs to grab hold of your awareness to do its bidding. But in your pause, you've judged there to be no real danger out there, just imperfection maybe, just a challenge to respond to. So you, by means of your pause, are saying "No" to the flare of frustration or fear or anger, or whatever dark feeling is rising. And you hold that pause steady. You make that pause as mighty a pause as you can. And you act like the clearest glass window onto your world to keep seeing what there is to see. And if you can hold on long enough…the onslaught from your limbic system will subside and quiet down.

What makes this process of breaking through, of breaking free of painful emotions, so very strange is that it goes on entirely within the confines of each person's own mind, as though it were going on inside of some kind of cocoon, hidden from the world.

Usually, anything that goes on inside quickly interacts with someone or something out there in the world. If we want to make a purchase, say, we feel the desire for it, and we proceed to seek it out in the world where the salespeople are, the shelves, the items, the money, etc. And if we feel mistreated or something is barring our way—an agency, a person, a physical barrier—we go out there and grapple with it. We speak into a phone or look into someone's eyes, or we lift or push or pull something. It's an old habit for our inner world to be busy responding to and interacting with the outer one.

But when there's emotional pain, chronically unrelieved by any of our efforts to reach into the physical world for a solution, we have to go and stay *inside*, and do something there. We let the world go except for basic needs and, perhaps, assistance in the form of a therapist, or a roadmap like this performance or other ones like it, to help light the way inside. And there we have the fateful encounter with the pain itself, the showdown with our own limbic system which is in a state of alarm, thinking with its negative emotion that there is real danger which isn't actually there. We try to quiet down the flaring of its emotion. And to do this we have to create a strong surge of strength in our awareness to hold still in that pause so we can be free to aim a steady, intensely observing, unshakeable force of disagreement right at the negative emotion flaring up from deep within our brain, which is frantically threatening to pull us, with its fast hypnosis, into a regrettable reaction or mood.

Nothing like this goes on in ordinary life. It's a biblical struggle. An old bondage is confronted. Before we are practiced and in command, a heavy, muscular conflict will occur. Inner energy will go against inner energy. A huge, twisting strain of a battle ensues in the deeply personal darkness of our own minds. And no one else will see it.

The problem: *inside*. All the work: *inside*.

Lights down.

Scene 27

It's True, We Have to Make an Unnatural Kind of Effort at First to Really Be in This Moment. We Do. But Do You Have Any Idea How Hard it was to Create This Moment? Really, it's the Least We Could Do.

At the beginning of the Big Bang, all the matter and energy was concentrated at the enormous temperature of 100 billion degrees Celsius!

Neil McAleer
The Cosmic Mind-Boggling Book (1982)

Lights come up.

[*Among other things in this scene, Consciousness thinks about parties and vacations and the easy life, and how hard it is almost always to make an effort to do something difficult. Hartman tries hard to read the gaze of Consciousness.*]

Throughout all of this talk about change, I'm not implying we're supposed to be spending *all* of our time trying to have huge emotional breakthroughs. Big, life-changing, personal breakthroughs are not events that occur regularly, like sunrises.

Breakthroughs are special developmental events, like learning how to walk, or speak, or read, which will reverberate in smaller ways for the rest of our lives. Someday when our culture makes it a high priority for its citizens to have healthy minds, emotional breakthroughs may become more customary, like bar and bat mitzvahs, confirmations, or baptisms. But maybe not so public, with all the guests, the dancing, and the partying. But they'll be acknowledged as special personal events—rites of passage for our awareness—marking an end and a beginning.

When a breakthrough happens for the first time, we turn away from ordinary, unselfconscious living. We separate ourselves from the world. We let the world go. We undertake something extraordinary, and it feels unnatural at first, so it's well worth repeating and describing in different ways. We go *inside* our minds—a strange, unaccustomed thing to do—and take our awareness to strange depths and distances in our brain to encounter the source of our pain. We go back to the wild primitive beginning of ourselves. We *see* and *feel*, maybe for the first time, how we can suddenly get pulled back by that old demanding, never-enough force inside (our limbic system), which is really our genetic inheritance and the repeated, long-neglected wound of our childhoods: the insistent yearning for emotional security and love that was threatened and disappointed more times than we can remember.

We overcome this wound by *seeing* it for what it is (overheated limbic activity), *knowing* that we are in different circumstances now, and *resisting* the way it pulls us with the fierce gravity of its dark opinion away from where we have to live right now. It is as though the soul of one part of the brain—you—begins to have a strong philosophical disagreement with the soul of another part—the limbic system—and, by means of a surge of confidence that there is no real danger that warrants such a flaring of negative emotion (anxiety, frustration, fear, anger, etc.), our awareness can effectively quiet it down and handle the outer situation more calmly, maybe even serenely. Inner energy against inner energy.

There's a sensation here of breaking free, of a kind of relationship, and a way of life, ending. We experience the thought, in more and more of our moments, that we can't go back to that way of falling so helplessly into our past, getting stuck feeling disappointment with what's around us and yearning away for a different world. We could be changed forever by not forgetting this. And as long as we can continue to activate our awareness in this way, maintaining that pause, the destabilizing reign of that old nerve center inside our brain will come to an end. We'll have the choice about drawing on its energy, weighing its opinion, instead of succumbing to it.

And when we return from this unusual journey, we can turn our attention, in a more carefree way, back to the world, sailing with the natural flowing of time through our lives without waiting to be taken care of by magic, which is what emotional pain is all about.

Then, when we're pulled back into the throes of a negative feeling—and we will surely be pulled back again—we'll remember the large effort we taught ourselves to make, and we'll know how to make a measure of it again.

How many moments do we each still have ahead of us? A self-defeating painful emotion could happen in any one of them. But each moment is also another opportunity for it not to happen the same way again.

Rarely, when we're living life day to day, do we aim ourselves so intensely in such a mysterious inner direction. We do it when we want to examine ourselves and when we're trying to change the way we feel and react to life. But maybe someday, when it's more widespread, this effort to activate our awareness and create this empowering pause will be incorporated somehow into our DNA and a quantum leap will have occurred in our evolution. It seems that such an improvement in our makeup as this can be installed with our (collective) will. We might then become a more comfortable, confident species. And it will mean, above all, transcending the tyranny of our basically innocent but haywire limbic system with which we have struggled with only limited success since civilization began.

Isn't it reasonable to think it might take an unusual kind of effort, at first, to overcome the deep pull of our painful emotions and experience more calmly a miracle like the present moment? Consider all the energy, concentration, heat—effort—that set time into motion in the first place, in order to bring us this moment?

Lights down.

Scene 28

The Innocence of the World, the Downright Blamelessness of the Whole Blasted Place. In Other Words, Ladies and Gentlemen, Our Emotional Pain is Not the World's Fault and Not Its Responsibility to Take Care of!

No snowflake ever falls in the wrong place.

Zen saying
Sunbeams (1990)

How we convince ourselves we have to go inside our minds, and go so deep we may need to vanish for a while

Lights come up.

[Among other things in this scene, Consciousness is a little amused watching Hartman step up the drama when he cups his hands and yells out, filling the theater with his voice, and also at the end when, by the way he quiets his voice, he creates the effect of disappearing into the recesses of a mind.]

To overcome the large and small emotional pains in life, we make it a practice to go back into our own minds and pause there. And there, in that pause, we can sense the desperate yearning preserved in the alarm of our painful emotion—an anguished cry to be loved and treated better and to feel more secure. We can see this in ourselves and all over the world in the international conflicts perpetually breaking out. And we also go into our minds and cultivate and strengthen that pause because it helps us to experience and grapple with the universe around us in this very moment. All of this, more or less, is what we're calling a breakthrough.

And when we go *inside* our brain with our pausing awareness and look carefully, we may notice that the surge of our negative feelings is responding, in an immediate, hypnotic way, to *the world outside.* We haven't ever scrutinized them very closely but they are locking us in a very unhealthy relationship with the world. That is, when we're in the very heat of a negative feeling, like frustration or embarrassment, don't we think it's due to someone or something *out there*? Or with a feeling like shame or guilt, we might blame ourselves, as though *we* could just as well be a culprit, like all the rest of them out in the world. Damned traffic! Damned prices! Damned greed! Damned mistake I made! Damned Fate! Damned whatever! In the heat of a negative emotion—and I mean momentarily while it's flaring through our minds, not when we've come to our senses—don't we believe somebody or something is to blame for screwing things up for us somehow and should be taking better care of us and our feelings? It's the neurological and historical nature of our limbic system to think that danger is coming from outside in our surroundings.

But if the truth is that we go *inside* our own brain to deal with the source of our unhappiness and work to free ourselves from the grip of our toxic negative emotions, and if we can actually become steady and serene by this effort, then how is it that we can go on holding the *outer* world responsible for any emotional pain we ever feel? We must be getting tricked somehow, unconsciously and quickly, into believing that the *outer* world is to blame and is responsible for us, but by something *inside* our brain that's casting a spell over us. And we might not even believe we're under this quick spell. But the strange quality of a spell is that we're not aware we're under it. And what it is that could cast such sudden spells like this inside our minds is that nerve network made of disappointed and threatened yearning (our limbic mind), and we may not realize it *while it's happening*.

So if our most far-reaching, empowering, steadying solution in life is to put our awareness to work *inside* our minds to handle our painful emotions, then we have to somehow stop believing the thought flaring through us that *the world* is responsible for it, that *the world* needs to be magically transformed from the way it is so that we can feel perfect and perfectly comfortable. It's this very thinking that is the problem, and it's this thinking we have to change. We have to stop damning the world and waiting in pain for the solution to come from it.

When it comes to the work that goes on inside a chrysalis, the caterpillar lets the world go. It takes complete responsibility for the job of making wings and turning into a butterfly. It's a decisive moment in the transformation of a caterpillar into a butterfly when it forms its chrysalis and separates itself from the world. The metamorphosis can't go on without this separation. There would be no butterflies at all if caterpillars kept waiting for the world to do the work of transforming them.

It's the same with us. It's crucial for us to believe the world is not the *cause* of our feelings of pain and unhappiness. People and circumstances in the world may *amplify* the pain that's already there inside our minds, but they don't *create* it, they don't *cause* it, and they can't be depended upon to relieve us of it in any lasting way.

Just as with the realization that our emotional pain comes from a completely different part of our brain than our awareness, this realization that the world is not the cause of our pain is also one of the most dramatic realizations and turning points we can have in our lives. It marks the beginning of the end of magical thinking that has insidiously plagued us. A new sense of responsibility for our feelings will surge into awareness. This shift can throw us off balance as we realize we have to handle things and steady ourselves. It can be very disorienting early on and we may be in some turmoil as we struggle with helplessness and uncertainty, and feel lost and alone, among other feelings.

And so, we often weaken under the impact of a negative feeling and blame the world for it because of the pained old yearning *inside* our minds to be loved and taken care of by our mothers or fathers, or somebody important, or by luck, or Santa Claus, or a superhero, or by the world, or God, or the whole cosmos. We fall under its spell, and believe that because she said this and he did this and that organization did that and this happened and that happened and that we don't get enough of this or that from here, there and everywhere, that *that's* why we're feeling our nasty emotion. We mistakenly believe the world is the real culprit here. We have it all wrong when we believe this. We have to call out to ourselves, shake ourselves free of this mistake in our thinking. I believe this is how we help ignite a real transformation.

We have to actually tell ourselves that it's natural to desire a solution to a problem or an obstacle we encounter in the world. It's natural, human, and very healthy. But if we don't desire that solution in a way that takes into account the limitations and possibilities in our immediate surroundings, we'll just fall back into magical ways of yearning for what we need, and our limbic system will direct our thinking and reactions. It'll flare up right through our awareness, the way a strong wind blows through a willow tree. And we'll strain with fear, worry, anger, hatred, or whatever feeling blows through us, depending on how badly we need a solution for what's going on out there right now. And it will sweep through us in ever stronger gusts all of our lives if we don't try to break its spell. So we have to start calling out to ourselves and keep calling out deeply and loudly. Actually, our culture would be a wonderful medium to hear this from, so amplified and influential its large voice can be:

"When painful emotions—strong negative feelings—are flaring right through your mind, overpowering you, you need to admit that your awareness is *not* the actual entity inside that's dealing with the world right now. The weakness in it is preventing that. You've fallen under a spell! You're being pulled back into the past by your limbic

system—that old pained yearning inside your brain for perfect love and security you never got! And you're getting stuck there! You're not really in the present anymore! You get pulled by it like there's no tomorrow—like there's no Now! And it's threatening to get you to react badly, believing the world is responsible!

"When this happens, you need to mobilize your strength and wake up from this spell! Free yourself from the grip of this old feeling! Pause, feel the emotion, don't act on it, just pause, hold steady, listen to its cry for magic, to that panic coming from deep inside your brain, wishing that what's out there would just disappear and be replaced by something better. Keep pausing!

and respond to the present moment in a more measured way! Not out of the demand for magic coming from the negative emotion!

"But when you've unwittingly fallen back into your past, with the old painful feeling flaring up, you may just get *angry* or *frustrated*. If you do, you've lost your strength! You might not even realize you're in the grip of this thing again—you just feel *angry* or *frustrated*—but these very feelings **mean** you're under its spell! You were pulled back so innocently, believing, with the force of the emotion, that the world is to blame for your problem, and that the world should have the solution, fix everything, and take care of you!"

It's a little strange to realize that what's going on right now out there in the world can make old feeling from the long ago inside our minds flare up, pull us back into its painful spell of needing to be rescued by magic, and completely control what we feel, think and do. We mustn't give up trying to awaken ourselves from it whenever it happens. We have to keep calling to ourselves, deeply and resonantly, until we're convinced of the truth and we can break the spell. Our culture ought to cup its hands around its mouth like a megaphone and call out to us even more loudly:

"The problem is not with what's going on in the world at all!! It's with the way you fall back into the past and the way your old, disappointed yearning for love and security flares up from deep inside your very own brain and holds you in its grip!! That's where the big problem is: inside your very own mind!! Not with the world!! The world is just a huge forest. You wouldn't expect a forest to take care of your painful emotions, would you? It's all just a huge, ever-changing forest out there to navigate and explore. Even people. Forests of people.

"No, you have to go to work inside, alone, and feel all the responsibility for yourself!!

"If necessary, you have to go further and deeper inside your brain than ever before and get to where the spell is coming from!! And you have to just hold still and stare it down!! Break yourself free from its influence and stop believing these things about the world!!

"You have to go inside now and do it yourself!! Make it happen!! You have to, alone!!"

This is what we have to say to ourselves and what our culture needs to say. And this is what caterpillars must communicate to themselves when they decide to form their chrysalises and get down to business. And as they keep working and working inside, an astounding and fateful moment comes to them from all of their labor: that quietest, blossoming instant when an idea that was never there before in its daily life gets stirred into its being and its living substance. And then, finally, it transcends its past and itself: It begins to grow wings and has created for itself the ability to fly.

For us humans, our bodies and lives are, for the most part, earthbound. But inside our minds, where there's just time, we fly as we can. We fly from image to image, from feeling to feeling, and from time to time. And we need to build a good, strong pair of wings in our awareness to do this well or we'll be thrown around like tumbleweed by the awful winds that can blow in there. And our wings grow the same way caterpillars grow theirs inside their chrysalises—an urgency to change drives the growth. An urgency to be able to get from there and then to here and now.

What we're all trying to do here in life, to achieve some kind of serenity, is break an exceedingly powerful old spell we've been under without ever fully knowing it. It flares up under different circumstances over and over again. Blaming the world is just another expression of this spell.

When we let the world off the hook and disappear into our minds to enshrine a pause, the present moment will be there for us to experience to the full with all of its strange and wondrous facts. We'll know how to steady ourselves in even the most trying moments of our lives. Because we won't need to be taken care of anymore. This will mark a major developmental shift in our being and a paradigm shift in our species. It could be so amazing. To see the present as it is, to glimpse its awesome depth and richness, without all of the painful yearning for magic and without blaming the world. We have to go inside now ... it could be amazing ... it could be amazing, Consciousness, amazing, ConsciousLadiesness **and Gentlemen** Consciousness, go deeper inside ... **Ladies and Gentlemen,** Consciousness, deeper and deeper ... **Ladies and Gentlemen** ... **And Ladies and Gentlemen ...**

Lights down.

Scene 29

And Now, Ladies and Gentlemen, I'd Like You All to Give a Warm Welcome to … The Present Moment! (Gasps, Oohs and Aahs, and Applause)

Quick now, here, now, always—

T. S. Eliot
Four Quartets (1943)

Lights come up.

[*Among other things in this scene, Consciousness thinks about dancing on a floor made of Jell-O.*]

Phht!

Here and gone, here and gone. Just like that.

The moment can go so fast.

Yet somewhere in this moment, somewhere in our awareness in this very moment, are truths about our human existence which, if we keep realizing them, can bring on the very deepest change.

"Just be in the moment," they say.

Sounds simple, huh?

Then why isn't everyone just doing it?

It's because there's no "just" about it. Look how fast the moment can come and go. Phht! And how elusive it is. Phht! And the chaos that can be in it.

Most of the time, we humans don't stop by an idea like "the present moment" long enough to understand it deeply. We're in the habit of moving too fast and carrying too big a load—assumptions, fantasies, expectations and yearnings of all kinds: to be loved, to be taken care of, to have control of things, to be verry special, and to keep holding onto moments, people, stuff, and grievances, forever and ever. We live this way with the belief that, somewhere in all of it, we'll find the meaning of our lives. And if by chance we glimpse it, we won't be able to enjoy it and live by it because we go barreling, with all of this freight, right through the present moment, hurtling toward the moment of paradise, or the paradise of moments, we're in search of.

The freight I'm talking about is none other than the hypnotic effects of the spell we're under from that past of ours, from that portion of the actual past that's as alive as the past could be and still be inside our minds right now. It's those wily, overheated amygdalae in our limbic system, suspended heavily and mightily there, trying to get control of us because they think they know better, flaring painful thoughts and feelings, darkening the inside with panic.

But the present moment is different from any of the moments we've collected in our minds, and different from our imaginings. It has a very distinct, unusual design to it. There are things that are urgently, seriously, fatefully true about the present moment, but we miss them.

One interesting thing that's true about the way we experience life is that we don't experience the sweep of decades that make up our lifetime. We only experience one moment at a time. We only experience Now. We can *think* the *thought* of a sweep of decades, but only in the span of *this* single moment.

And there's only one real present moment—only one. It's always here for us, and yet every present moment that passes away is also gone for good. Always here and always passing away. Our entire existence is always contained within this moment right now. Any imagining we do about the future, we do now, and any memory we recall from the past, we recall right now. This moment is it. There's no other moment. Here it is. And now it's gone for ever. And here it is again.

And we also outlive the present moment. Each present moment becomes a tiny afterlife of the previous moment that passed away. Each present moment comes and goes, and we live on. And then there we are, right in the middle of the present moment again.

Trying to understand the truth about the moment can be like trying to dance on a floor made of Jell-O. Our mind keeps wobbling around on the idea.

To be in this moment, we just can't barrel through it. We have to slow down and notice it. And what we're doing when we realize this is, in effect, becoming at odds with this inner pressure we're under. We pause and begin a disagreement with our limbic mind. We try to break its spell over us, the same way we work to stop blaming the world for what's happening to us in life. **This sort of spell-breaking protest is a crucial activity our awareness engages in during a breakthrough**. For instance, instead of complaining about the bleakness of a rainy day, we activate ourselves to protest against the ridiculous demand inside our minds that the rainy day not be there. We protest against a part of our very own mind *thinking* the wrong way, instead of blaming the world for raining. We accept the rainy day completely, and accept our experience of it. We soak it up, and maybe we even sing and dance in it.

What we're ultimately doing through this inner disagreement is pulling our awareness away from the grip of this old overactive, troubled part of our brain. It's something akin to generating enough force to resist the pull of Earth's gravity and fly free, making it possible to experience new kinds of feelings that can blend together into a long-lasting, deliciously complex calm called serenity. And pausing is where serenity begins.

By serenity, I don't mean some nirvana we go to, or heaven, or oblivion. I just mean a blend of new feelings that arise from what's simply true about right now. Serenity is an interesting blend of facts about Now and the corresponding qualities of character, all working together that hold us steady, like wings do in air, so we can be attentive to the moment and move around in it in an interesting new way, free from the grip of the pain from our past.

When we can do this, we've done a radical thing. We've given up the idea that any two moments are alike. And we come to a kind of halt at each new moment, sort of at the entrance to each moment, and we realize, ever so briefly, that each moment has a completely different universe in it, with possibilities different from any other moment, wherever we are and whatever is happening. And there may also be the slightest little ache which accompanies this halt, because no matter how much of the moment we are able to take in, it passes so quickly that we only get the merest hint of its vastness, its potential, and its magnificence.

So being in the present moment means not only accepting what's true about it (scenes 30 through 36) and how we keep trying to stabilize ourselves in it, but also how well we're able to keep pulling ourselves out of the grip of our distorting past, without forgetting where we've been.

To be in this moment means being prepared to make this little odyssey by ourselves, whenever necessary, through all the time inside our mind, from then to Now.

In the silence of our minds, without anyone ever knowing what we're doing there, we work to shape our awareness into a strong, lucid, vibrant pause—because this is exactly what the present moment feels like at its best, when we're not in danger, which is almost every moment.

This is how we can resonate with it.

This is how we can empathize with it,
slowly.

Actually, Now is the birthplace of awareness.

The only present moment there is has just arrived, also just like a newborn. And my my, it won't be here for long...

And it's so much more wondrous than getting caught like a hostage by the awful gravity of old feeling.

And my my, it's never here for long...

But here it is...

And we can have the whole, stupendous thing,
complete with a moving universe,
with its strange collection of facts, truths, decisions, destinies, mysteries, all perfect and so imperfect...
Phhhhhhhhhhhhhhhhhhhhhhhhhhhhhhhhhhhhhhhhhhhhhhhhhhht!

Lights down.

Here are Seven Routes You Could Take Out of the Pain in Your Past and into the Serenity in This Moment. They Were Found by a Search Party of Thousands Scouring the Higher and Lower Elevations in My Office.

Why time is other than time was.

W. H. Auden
No Time (1940)

Lights come up.

[Human Consciousness always enjoys a good countdown.]

Okay, the seven scenes that follow describe facts about the present moment which, I believe, are ingredients to help expand a pause into a deeper experience of serenity. They're Facts. No, they're laws. No, being in the present moment is like a game you play in, and they're the rules to the game. When you want to play a game well, you have to accept certain rules about it. Accepting the rules means you give up other possibilities so you can achieve a certain kind of experience—like the rules of playing baseball, or the rules of performing heart surgery, or the rules of space flight. You have to obey the rules or you won't enjoy the effect of the game; it won't be any fun, or be healing, or be awe-inspiring.

So here come the facts I've gathered, the rules for a calm transit through the present moment of time. There are seven of them that I could find. And like the rules of baseball or spaceflight, they all work together. One might seem to apply better than another in a particular instance, but they all really apply at the same time. They all add up to define the game. The rules of the game are the game, just as those seven colors making up the rainbow, blending in different ways, are what illuminate the universe.

I don't believe serenity is just a simple, quiet feeling, although it appears that way because there is a peacefulness in it. Like light, it is a blend of distinct things that are true. So it's not just sitting on a lawn chair, sipping iced tea and enjoying the view. It could be that. I'm referring to a species of serenity you feel while in the very thick of things, in the crush and heave of life.

I believe a way into this kind of serenity is by accepting each fact about the nature of the present moment, each rule for playing in it. You learn and study each unexpected rule. You grow into each mysterious one—then, with a gathering effort, into all of them together at once. And the paradigm will shift, as on a space flight, or up among all those soft colors glowing and dissolving in a rainbow—and you just become light.

Lights down.

Scene 30

1. Recognizing that the Present Moment is Here Right Now in All of Its Mystery and Splendor and Challenge. Feeling Courage as You Go to Encounter it

Courage mounteth with occasion.

William Shakespeare
King John (1594–1596)

The occasion for us—the only occasion, ever—is Now.

What you can't get out of, get into wholeheartedly.

Mignon McLaughlin
The Neurotic's Notebook (1963)

And what we can't get out of—until we die—is Now.

Lights come up.

[*Among other things in this scene, Consciousness almost laughs imagining Hartman, with his cowboy hat on, riding a bucking bronco at a rodeo.*]

One of the simplest things you could find to think about right now is that the present moment is here right now. It feels like a large pause out there, built into nature, that allows us to move around in it and live. Although the work of the brain may have a lot to do with this moment feeling the way it does, it's also the size and speed of the spinning and revolving Earth that determines the shape of it. And you don't need to look that far to feel the presence of the moment. But the farther out you do look, the more immense, mysterious, and challenging you begin to realize it is. It's not something inside our minds, like our past. It is actually there. And it's not just a thin little boundary line separating an immense past from a boundless future. The present moment feels like it is everything.

Now is actually every moment of time that ever was and ever will be. *Now* was the past when the past was happening, and *Now* is the only way we know that the past is past. *Now* holds all of our speculation about the future, and *Now* will *be* the future when it happens. We spend our entire lifetime in this one, single moment called *Now*. It is our only living moment.

Then there are those nasty spells cast by our negative feelings which flare up out of our pasts. They're all still there, collected inside our minds— spells like:

irritation,   **ANNOYANCE,**   **ANGER**,   **PANIC**,

DEPRESSION, or **MISERY**.

These feelings sweep through us hypnotically and try to sway us to reject the present moment, because where they come from inside our brain is feeling afraid for us. These negative feelings actually seek to eliminate the present moment and everything in it (which is everything there is). They make us believe, in a rush, that this moment right now is not good for us, that it could and should be replaced with a much better Now.

And as we succumb to these spells of emotions, we get thrown. But then we're back in the moment, and then we're thrown again when another negative emotion flares up, because of how vulnerable our awareness is to old yearnings for perfect love and security, which are preserved in these negative feelings. Then we'll find ourselves right back in the present moment again. None of our painful emotions ever change the present moment; they're only ineffective revolts against it. This moment is inescapable, no matter what illusion we put ourselves under, no matter what we wish or dream or need or demand.

The present moment is big, really big and powerful, just like our limbic system, which was forged by fierce threats to life in so many present moments far back in our evolution. And the present moment also moves fast and doesn't care if we're on it or not. So it would be best if we could learn to ride it well, accept its presence, understand the strange conditions it imposes on us, and work with it as it is—and tame this jumpy, panicky limbic system of ours.

When European Americans moved into the western frontier of North America in the eighteenth and nineteenth centuries, they were challenged to the core of their beings by the hardships and threats they found there. A communal spectacle was eventually invented to grapple with it. It was an athletic event that summed up what they were all facing, and what they needed to find in themselves to prevail in their harsh circumstances: courage, independence of spirit, a sense of responsibility, single-minded focus, the right sense of humility in the face of a challenge, and the tenacity to keep holding on. The event was the rodeo, and the heroes were the rodeo cowboys and cowgirls, trying to hold steady on wild horses bent on trying to throw them off. The horse was symbolic of the West, which was wild, unpredictable, dangerous, and potentially overwhelming. To handle it, you had to keep your head and your balance, or you were done for.

The present moment and our limbic system—both can be wild in the ways the American West once was. The present moment is loaded with the unknown, and with the potential for what can evoke terror and other jarring emotions that can throw us off, but also with the potential for triumph and fulfillment. It's loaded with what humbles and inspires.

All we need in order to handle this moment is to conjure in our awareness the feeling that we're ready for it, a strong quiet feeling of courage as we go to encounter it, even though the moment is huge and mysterious and we don't know exactly what's going to happen, what twists and turns we're in for, and what will jar us from within.

As our awareness keeps emerging into this only living present moment, what we do to be ready is to make a habit to halt, ever-so-slightly, at the beginning of it. In other words, we slow down. We fill our awareness with a readiness. We turn our awareness into the feeling of courage itself, measured enough for the moment—a very daring thing to do in the face of any encounter with the unknown.

And turning into things is, after all, the way awareness works. Our awareness turns into perceptions, feelings, thoughts, attitudes, and beliefs that add up to experiences in life, and then lets them all go. They fall into our minds, where they're collected. Then our awareness can recollect them or it can go on to turn into new perceptions, feelings, thoughts, attitudes, and beliefs, and have new experiences, and in this way we build our lives. That's what's so astounding about us, about our awareness: it's an amazing, responsive material that can absorb, and sort of become, so much of what it's exposed to.

But this astounding responsiveness can work against us if we're not careful and strong. Our awareness can also succumb to the pained yearning for magic and perfection that comes from deep inside our brains, which can flare right through us whenever we hit obstacles in life, like traffic, disease, or the imperfection of things, or when someone doesn't do exactly what we want them to do. And then, when our awareness is at the end of its strength and resourcefulness, these old feelings take over and commandeer our lives in this only moment we have. The intense need and demand in them impair our attitudes, our decisions, our behavior, and our outlook on life. They also lead us to feelings of regret and shame over our loss of control and the mishandling of our moments.

When it comes to having a healthy mind, the name of the game is more freedom to choose what your awareness will and won't turn into. We may not be able to prevent the initial blasts of feeling that flare up from our limbic system and through our awareness, because we're human, and we have this past inside that can flare this way. But we can strengthen our awareness enough to maintain a firm boundary between us and these limbic feelings and hold on tight to the feeling we choose. It'll change the whole texture of our lives in the present moment. And it'll also decisively change the kind of memories we're creating and storing away. The memory of a feeling of courage has a very different, far-reaching, strengthening effect on the interior of our minds, compared with a memory of helplessness, fear, anger, or hatred.

We really don't need to know a thing well at all, like the present moment, to have the courage to deal with it, to be ready for it. And we don't have to worry about a perfect ride. A perfect ride is not up to us. This moment is big and powerful. All we have to do is be as ready for it as we can be and make the effort to hold on.

The first ingredient of that mighty calm called serenity is the *feeling of courage* that arises from accepting that the present moment is simply here, right now, in all of its challenge. When we blend this ingredient with the other six ingredients described ahead, it will help to steady our awareness, just for this present moment—the crossroads into the future—which is all we need to do to begin to set our lives, and our world, on a different course.

Lights down.

Scene 31

2. Giving Up Your Yearning to be Loved in All of the Ways You Were Never Loved Enough as a Child.
Learning New Ways of Love

No one has ever loved anyone the way everyone wants to be loved.

Mignon McLaughlin
The Neurotic's Notebook (1963)

Lights come up.

[*Among other things in this scene, Consciousness thinks about love, that feeling of being in love, and about what Hartman might have been like as a young man when he was madly in love.*]

This very moment we're in right now is unlike any that has ever happened. If you look around, you can sense how different it is, how much you don't know about it. It's new. It's one of a kind. There's never been anything like it. Never happened before. Never happen again. Each moment is a kind of break with the past, and doesn't really follow from the one before it. Each moment is its own vast universe, its own one-of-a-kind arrangement of the cosmos.

I've been making the case that the flaring of a negative feeling (resentment, loneliness, etc.) is a mute old cry in our minds for a more perfect kind of love and security. I claim that this cry comes right out of our past that's still inside our minds, right out of our limbic system. It flares up into awareness, violating its boundary, and sears it with pained old yearning whenever we hit an unacceptable obstacle and lose our strength to deal with it. The present moment, the universe out there, can be indifferent to this cry. In fact, the very surge of our negative feeling implies that this cry to be taken care of differently—to be loved perfectly—is being disregarded by the circumstances we're facing right now.

But the present moment is not there to take care of us. It's not your mother, or my mother. If anything, it's more like a bucking bronco than a mother. But the primitive limbic feeling from our past doesn't know this and can't accept it. Only our awareness is in a position to accept this.

So the present moment sits quietly, full of its mystery. Or it clamors its way into our lives, full of just as much mystery. Whatever potential it has to love us, to give us a pleasing and fulfilling experience, is not at all clear. Yet the assumption deep inside our minds is that this potential to love us ought to be endless. Our old, inner need for perfect love assumes that the present moment very definitely will bring that special love—until it doesn't and won't. Then, upon the clash, the old painful disappointment that's welded to this yearning flares high into our minds and we reject our surroundings while we yearn, and so we suffer.

Our job as humans is to find out what the present moment has to offer, and what it doesn't. We can't know this instinctively. We can't assume. We need to *see*, with our clear, free awareness, what's possible and what's not.

To be in *this* very moment, to handle its sheer, mysterious presence and be as calm and steady as we can be, we have to give up needing to be loved, especially in the ways we weren't loved enough as kids. But we don't give up remembering this past. We just work to resist the pull of this inflamed feeling in our limbic system so we can deal with this one huge moment we're in right now.

And we may not even be aware we need this love and security. We're not even aware, as our pain flares randomly through our days, that an old yearning for love is crying out in this pain. We don't necessarily communicate it to ourselves in these terms. We've been under its spell all of our lives, and our culture hasn't helped us very much with this just yet. We're not used to thinking twice about it.

So we may not even realize all of this is going on in our lives as much as it is. And we may not be able to call it the largest and worst problem we have.

So to be in *this* moment is to be somewhere we've never ever been before. It means being prepared to get our balance and take in the new landscape. Then we can explore it and determine what it can or cannot give us, before we go assuming, expecting, or demanding anything.

Just look around right now. Look at how ambiguous and enigmatic it is. It's everywhere you look. And there really isn't much time for assumptions, expectations, and demands, anyway. Before we know it, the moment's gone, and then there we are again in another moment, facing another universe full of more unknowns.

No, the present moment is not our mother, or our father, or our grandma or grandpa or our special aunt or uncle, or our very favorite TV show. It's more like a bucking bronco. And at its most trying moments, it's like the bucking bronco of all bucking broncos. And we're always right up there on it, always being released from that chute. And we have to keep our priorities very simple to hang on and keep ourselves out of the dust.

If we can accept all of this and break the old spell of pain that flares from inside—and not damn what we have unless we're facing real danger or a threat to our lives—our minds could begin to open. And we might notice, and calmly, that there are other new kinds and shades of love to recognize in unexpected places.

The love and security we find may not be like what we missed so much as kids. It probably won't be. It will likely be very different, because we'll be busy keeping our own balance and handling things for ourselves. It may be simpler than we thought. It may be more subtle. And it may not announce itself as love at all. It may be as simple as looking at the sunlight slanting in, or the moonlight falling. Or it may be in noticing all the gray that can be out there. We may actually find it there in all of that gray. Or we might find love in the mere presence of someone, just simply in the awareness that he or she is there. Or we may actually end up discovering love in the whole way we're being thrown by life and how we're handling the challenge to hold on. Who knows? But it will be very real. And it will always be right before our eyes.

The second ingredient of serenity is the *opening of awareness* to new unexpected ways to love.

Lights down.

Scene 32

3. Believing You are Alone Inside Your Own Mind Right Now. Cultivating Inner Security and Self-Reliance

Alone, alone, all, all alone,
Alone on a wide wide sea!

Samuel Taylor Coleridge
The Rime of the Ancient Mariner (1798)

Lights come up.

[*Among other things in this scene, Consciousness thinks about the possibility of speaking, if it weren't for who and what (s)he is, which is pure awareness, and about the idea that (s)he could be taking Hartman seriously or not seriously at all and he might not have any idea what was being thought.*]

Look around in this moment right now and you can notice not only that the moment is here, and that you're in it, but that you're alone. You're completely alone right now, sort of separate from the rest of your mind and everything else.

I'm not diminishing the value and power of the closeness we can have with others. Yet if you think about the complexity of any of the moments in your day, a human relationship is really but one small element among so many.

But it doesn't matter wherever you are or whomever you're with. When you're out there in life, you're *inside your mind*, alone. I mean in a physical, anatomical way. No one's ever there inside with us, and no one ever will be.

It's possible for there to be a simultaneous concern resonating among large numbers of people at once, making it seem as though we're extended beyond the confines of our single mind. But the substance of our awareness remains inside, generated from the one human mind and brain we are each within.

Awareness is solitary; it travels alone from birth to death. No one knows for sure where you are inside right now, how far back in time you're getting pulled by memory and emotion, and what kind of pain you're feeling. No one knows what you're thinking or imagining, or how serene you may be feeling. You're alone with all of that.

And I don't mean lonely. It's our limbic system, or whatever it might be called someday, which flares old painful states into us, pulling that important boundary apart between it and our awareness, that makes us feel lonely. It's our limbic system which can pull us way back into the old illusion that we badly need a certain kind of company, or everlasting security, or the immediate fulfillment of all of our dreams, which makes us believe that we are empty, not full. We need to become more stressed about this illusion and the sorcery behind it. We need to become so stressed about it, so opposed to it, that we shatter its spell and restore calm in our awareness.

So what I'm saying here is something that's just simply true: we're each alone inside our minds right now. Just simply alone in there. And we always will be. It's not a bad thing. It just is. It's just the way we each ride through life.

And if we can simply realize and accept that, in this fundamental sort of way, we're inescapably alone for our entire lives, then we're in a position to cultivate a new kind of inner security and self-reliance in this moment that can help to stabilize our awareness and our lives. Just realizing and embracing this fact can help us to give up the urge to escape from it, and it can galvanize an acceptance of our circumstances, a very basic kind of acceptance of our human situation. And only then, when we're comfortable with our fundamental separateness in life, can we enjoy and express our unique perspective of the world, and only then can we become truly intimate with another person.

So we build this inner security and self-reliance knowing that we must. No one else is there, or ever will be there, to provide it. Even God, for those who believe God may be inside our minds with us, would require us to build this inner security and self-reliance in the pure freedom of our will.

Just as our universe itself is expanding into the unknown at the speed of light, each of us is on our own fast ride through life, seeking our own unique and solitary embrace of the mystery before us.

The third ingredient of serenity is the *feeling of self-reliance and inner security* that grows out of accepting the fact that you are alone inside your mind right now.

Lights down.

Scene 33

4. Accepting that You are Completely Responsible For the Care and Condition of Your Own Consciousness Right Now. Building Competence

I've got two words to say to you: Cowboy up.

from the movie
8 Seconds (1993)

Lights come up.

[*Among other things in this scene, Consciousness thinks that, underneath any gentleness and sensitivity, Hartman is actually a little hardened and stoical.*]

So far, I've stated that there is such a thing as our present moment, that we're each in our own right now, and that in order to be in it well, we have to find a way to overcome the pull of our old childhood need for perfect love and security and then experience new kinds of love and security. And if it's true that we're each completely alone inside our own mind right now, then it must also be true that, to be as steady as possible in this strangely beautiful interval we experience called the present moment (the only interval there is), we each have to take full responsibility for the care and condition of our own awareness right now.

Not talking about blame or perfection. Not saying we always have to feel perfectly serene and be Zen masters. That would be nice. Just saying that something will come along that isn't to our liking, and we may feel like we haven't the strength to deal with it. Our limbic system will pull hard with its old yearning, and then an intensely unpleasant, needy, disappointed feeling will flare through us. We'll fall under its spell and tumble back into its chaos. And I'm saying it's our high responsibility to handle this situation inside. It's no one else's. It's each of ours, alone.

Here's another way of suggesting the truth about this that may be helpful to some:

Who do you think would take responsibility for the feeling you're feeling right now?! That feeling is emanating from brain tissue very close to where you happen to be right now! Do you think someone else should do it, and actually could?!

It's a bit of time travel we each have to do. From the grip of the emotion from the bygone past in our limbic mind into the wild immensity of Now. And we're each responsible for our own journey. Awareness is the pilot. Our awareness is what has to respond to the inner and outer situation it finds itself in—respond, responsive, responsible. Since our awareness is alone inside our minds, it's the only thing that knows what the situation is inside and what needs to be done about it.

It's certainly an odd dilemma to find ourselves inside of a mind, in this universe, in this moment called Now. It's odd always having to realize and accept that we can't count on being loved in the ways we were and weren't loved enough as kids. And it's odd always having to embrace the ideas that we're each so alone inside our mind and so responsible for handling the strange little miracle that is our own awareness.

But when we can finally fully accept that we are completely responsible for whatever awareness we have, we can learn what we need to learn to handle it: truths, ideas, practical know-how. And this can galvanize a kind of faith in ourselves, which is just a strong feeling of *competence* that we can and will be able to handle our own awareness.

So we have to commit ourselves to learn to pilot this awareness which we are, and which we possess, out of that past of ours, out of the grip of our limbic system, and free ourselves from the overpowering feeling that someone or something else is responsible for us. We each alone put together all of the necessary ideas and gather the wing power we need. We each take our responsibility for learning what to fly away from inside our minds, and what to fly toward, and how to maneuver ourselves through all of the tricky terrain in between.

This effort we make by ourselves inside to build our own philosophies of life and the skills to steady ourselves, is the *only* source of self-confidence there is in the known universe.

The fourth ingredient of serenity is the *feeling of competence* that develops from accepting responsibility for the care and condition of your own awareness right now.

Lights down.

Scene 34

5. Admitting that You Don't Know Very Much about Very Much, Especially Right Now. Experiencing Wonder

The Delphic Oracle said that I was the wisest of all the Greeks.
It is because I alone of all the Greeks know that I know nothing.

Socrates (469–399 BC)
Sunbeams (1990)

Lights come up.

[*Among other things in this scene, Consciousness gazes out the window for a while, daydreaming about all the water that was found on the Moon and thinking the sweet thought that it may mean life is everywhere out there and that the universe might just be teeming with consciousness. Hartman modulates his tone, trying to stir up Consciousness, as he watches Consciousness gaze past him.*]

Another striking thing that's true about the present moment is how profoundly mysterious it is. Into this moment you take the fund of information you've acquired in life. But how much knowledge is that really, given the size of this moment and the cosmos it's filled with? How much of what could be known do we know? And how much do we know about what's going on *right now*?

What we get from the news coming out of the media amounts to the most infinitesimal speck of what's really going on out there. It leaves out almost the entire human universe, let alone the non-human one. Just think of what's happening everywhere else on the planet: in people's homes, inside every single mind, and in nature. And what about what's going on beyond the planet? And how many dimensions are there in the universe? And how many universes are there?

And as far as the so-called hard facts of science go, just look at what becomes of them as you go through history. They get hauled into the big antique shop of human thought. And I'm not saying that pursuing knowledge is a bad thing. It's a truly wonderful thing. It makes for great gadgets, like wheels and computers, that help us out in all sorts of ways. It can be very exciting, like finding water on the Moon or learning that stars are all water factories. But we shouldn't be fooled into believing that we ever really know very much about very much, especially about what's going on in *this* moment right now. Continually being added to every moment is something unknown that keeps nullifying any complete certainty we can ever have about anything. So if we're going to be in tune with the moment before us, we need to add a respect for the unknown to any conviction we might be inclined to have about what we think we know for sure.

At the more personal level, no one else but you knows what's going on inside your own mind right now. Even you might not know. And you don't know much about what anyone else is thinking. Don't be fooled by the cheers or the boos coming from the human audience out there. Sure, you might be able to identify a thought or two sweeping through the crowd. But even a single human mind is vast, let alone the mind of an audience; it has more going on in it than we could ever imagine. No, what's there right now in anyone's mind has a complexity to it that is way beyond any absolute certainty we can ever have about it. All we can have are our hunches.

And if we can bring ourselves to believe deeply that, in the whole scheme of things in *this* moment, we actually know very little about anything, it leads to one of the most pleasurable, freeing experiences a human can have: wonderment.

I'm not saying we can't study and know those facts we've learned and need to know for our test tomorrow, or how to make a soufflé, or how to operate all of the electronic and mechanical contraptions in our lives. I'm talking about putting all of this into a larger context and wondering right through all of the so-called facts. Wonderment comes when we can free ourselves from the grip of *needing* to know for sure, and from the grip of being convinced that we do know—and realizing by ourselves, inside our own minds, what enormous mystery there is and always will be in this moment and every other one.

This can also lead us to a very interesting and freeing implication when it comes to our relationships with people. If it's true that, in this moment, our knowledge is more limited than we think, and if there's so much mystery to reckon with everywhere we look, can we really take anything too personally? If we know far less than a tiny bit about what's really going on anywhere right now, how sure can we really be that events, words, or actions are meant personally for you or me, however focused on us they might appear to be? Shouldn't there be at least a little doubt about taking it too personally, no matter how unfortunate it is, or how mean someone sounds, or even how loving? Something else may be going on in the process, and we might not know about it. I'm not saying we can dismiss misfortune, love, or hate we perceive being directed at us. We'll need to deal with it somehow. I'm saying there's probably much more to it than we might easily conclude.

I'm saying that our limited knowledge can give us pause to wonder, a pause full of wonder, a wonderful pause, filled with the simplest, quietest, most curious awareness of right now.

So when you're trying to hold on to and tame that bucking, heaving limbic system inside and the universe outside, it all comes down to knowing how to find your own center of gravity and knowing how to hold it as steady as you can. Knowing anything else is neither here nor there.

The fifth ingredient of serenity is the *feeling of wonderment* evoked by accepting how little we actually know about what's going on anywhere and everywhere right now.

Lights down.

Scene 35

6. Acknowledging that You are Very Insignificant and Inessential in the Whole Scheme of Things. Becoming Humble

Humility, like darkness,
reveals the heavenly lights

Henry David Thoreau
Walden (1854)

Lights come up.

[Among other things in this scene, Consciousness thinks Hartman would like to hold the whole universe in his hands.]

We are somewhere inside a universe that's about 14 billion light-years deep. It may contain as many as 2 trillion galaxies, each casting the light of about 100 billion stars. Plus there's the other *96%* of the universe made of Cold Dark Matter and Dark Energy. Fourteen billion huge light-years full of the light and the dark! So how significant can we each be in all of this? Very? Or very not.

Now let's go to a smaller scale and get another sense of our significance. Let's go to the level of our atoms, or within our atoms. There's actually practically nothing there at all. The particles that are there, flashing in and out of existence, are separated by vast distances on that scale. At that level there's mostly just empty space reaching in every direction. What's to be significant or insignificant there?

Now let's look at the in-between scale, to the level of our senses and our common sense way of thinking. Here's where we're fooled the most about how significant we really are. Let's consider an extreme scenario to heighten the effect. Say that while you're in this moment, you're also a pilot. The passengers are depending upon you for their lives, right? In a way, and for a while. So you're very significant. Rather, what is significant about you is your know-how and the way you use your awareness to fly the plane. The rest of you doesn't matter here, either. And after the plane lands, then how significant are you?

So there are those moments in life when you're vital, in a brief, mechanical sort of way, for the physical safety of someone else. But when you don't happen to be in control of those physical forces and machines people's lives depend upon—which is most of the time—you're even physically insignificant and inessential. And what if the plane went down? It would be a terrible tragedy. But think of the 14 billion light-years worth of universe out there or even the gigantic sweep of human history alone. Then how significant, really, is a terrible tragedy in the entire scheme of things? What is a plane going down, compared with the light and dark of 14 billion lights-years worth of universe and all the time yet to come? The universe would go on without you, the plane, and the passengers. It would go on and on until it doesn't anymore.

And think of your significance in the distant future. Let's say a hundred years from now. Even if you did something very memorable in the public eye, you would long ago have turned into a myth or a legend. The brief music of your name would be associated with the memorable thing you did, but no one would know who *you* really were—*you*, the complex, mysterious, psychological being right now made of living awareness with a vast, unique, private warehouse of old moments, imagery, and feeling. And how significant would you be in two hundred years, or two thousand or twenty thousand? Whatever was known about you would fade into oblivion in a short time.

In the colossal ocean of time and space that is the universe, we are the tiniest specks. We come and go like subatomic particles. We're specks that are largely forgotten, specks that are never really known at all. The present moment is always bringing in change and adding the unknown. Each one of us is pulsing away in our own mysterious system and handling our own enigmatic moment. Psychologically, we could vanish into dementia, move to another part of the country, or die, and aspects of us might be badly missed. But the entire world would go on without us, and quickly. No one needs us to be there. So it may sound like a nice idea to think we're significant, but there's just too much space and time and mystery out there to support this.

This is not to imply that life isn't precious, or that anyone should feel defeated or inadequate. I'm not trying to diminish the sacredness of human life or how important our own awareness is and should be to each of us. I'm offering a perspective, a context beyond how we usually see ourselves. I find this useful in helping someone achieve a more realistic perspective about being in the present moment, especially when we're in the throes of painful needs to be more significant than we are or can be.

It's that old mass of threatened feeling, our limbic system, amping up our need to be so significant, enchanting us into believing we ought to be much more significant in the eyes of other people. It keeps saying to each of us, while we're getting whirled around on that present moment, that other people and institutions ought to know how important and special we are. The universe filling this present moment should know how much we're worth and treat us accordingly. But no.

We're profoundly insignificant in the scheme of things. And when we can accept how true this is—without feeling at all inadequate about this fact—we will have freed ourselves from the pull of those old feelings in our minds. We will have helped to reinforce the boundary between us and our limbic system. We'll be freer to understand why people might not treat us the way we wish they would. We'll be able to wonder enough to understand that there are reasons which very likely have little or nothing to do with who we really are, because we're simply not that important. And isn't that wonderful? Isn't it all so humbling?

So if someone gets mad because he or she isn't liking the way you are right now, and you're not really hurting anyone, then it's not your fault. It's probably the workings of the limbic system getting amplified inside that person's own mind; some unrealistic yearning and disappointment of their own at work—needing to be loved the way *they* were never loved enough as kids. You're not the cause of it. The real cause of someone else's feeling is always inside his or her own mind. And by the way, if you do fail to do something you believe you should have done, you can say you're sorry, feel it deeply, show it sincerely, and try to prevent it from happening again. And that's that.

What I'm after in all of this is to enlarge our perspective enough so that it, in effect, shrinks the size of our *painful need for significance*, cooling our emotion down to the simplest, humblest, most responsive awareness of being fully alive somewhere in the universe.

The sixth ingredient of serenity is the *feeling of humility* arising from the realization of our insignificance in the grand scheme of things.

Lights down.

Scene 36

7. Realizing that You Even Have to Let Go of the Present Moment, Too. Developing a Healthy Capacity for Sorrow

Parting is such sweet sorrow,
That I shall say good night till it be morrow.

William Shakespeare
Romeo and Juliet (1594)

Lights come up.

[*Among other things in this scene, Consciousness thinks about the end of psychotherapy again, when and what will happen.*]

And finally, the very last thing that's simply true about the present moment, which you can verify from where you're sitting right now, is this: that even this moment itself will pass away. It, and everything in it, will be gone for good. All of it will go.

Your limbic system doesn't much like this idea. It doesn't think this way. It runs on magic, not reality, and it wants pleasure and fulfillment to last forever. It's not interested in things passing away. It wants to be loved forever. It wants security forever because it's so often worried that we're not safe, even when we are. It wants to hold on forever. It wants to dream about forever, forever. It doesn't want anything to end, ever. That thing in your mind is all about forever and ever and never enough, ever.

But Now is all about never again. Change is just about all that happens in life. Being fully in this very moment also means letting it go and accepting that we will never have it again in all of its perfect or imperfect fullness.

We'll have the tiniest trace of it to carry in our possession called a memory. But a memory is not a moment like Now. Far from it. It's infinitesimally smaller. And no two moments will ever be alike. That's not the way time works. Each moment carries its own universe. Each moment is total and will pass totally away.

So we'll never again be exactly the same way we are right now. The way we're being tossed and thrown by life and the way we keep our balance will never again be as it is now. And all the humans around us will never respond again exactly the way they're responding to us right now.

Whether we choose to acknowledge it or not, there's a subtle sense of loss we could feel as each present moment passes away, however ordinary the moment might be.

And the feeling that can come from our awareness of this continual loss of the present moment is a kind and very small degree of sorrow. This feeling is the healthiest feeling of pain there is. You won't find it on that long list in scene 9. It's not there because the feelings on that list come from those old masses of moments in our amygdalae deep inside our brain, that pull on us like mad to *reject* the present moment because it believes we're in danger.

Sorrow is different. Sorrow has intimations of acceptance stirring within it. It implies a wish that things *might* be different, but are the way they are, and have to be the way they are and then have to pass away because of forces that are much more powerful than we'll ever be. So in this healthy hint of sorrow, you surrender your embrace of each moment as time carries it away, and you forgive all—the universe and you—for all the limitations that were in that moment, all of the imperfection and incompleteness. Then you're free to embrace and reckon with the next new moment materializing before you. And this sorrow we feel about all of the limitations we always face wouldn't weaken any efforts we strive to make. As a bridge to acceptance, this ever-so-subtle feeling of sorrow could help take us closer to the healthiest limits of the efforts we can make in life, free from the disabling pressure of all of those other painful emotions, which are always rejecting the limits. It can help us to seize the moment and work the best we can with what we have while we have it. Our sorrow helps us to move along in the ceaseless flowing of time and participate as intimately as possible as each moment blossoms and fades along the way.

And sorrow is also what completes our serenity, the way violet completes the rainbow. The feeling of sorrow has a weight to it, a steadying weight. It tells us the rodeo of life will end someday, and it is all right. The present moment will be gone forever. The ride is going to end someday for me, for you. Everything is going to pass away: our whole life, our last breath ... but the truly immense thing, passing away most profoundly of all, right before our eyes, is Now. And it is all right.

The seventh ingredient of serenity is the *feeling of sorrow* that comes from realizing that the present moment, with everything in it, is passing away right now, and you have to let it all go.

Lights down.

Scene 37

So You Think these Seven FACTS about Being in the Present Moment Sound Grim? Are You Kidding Me? I'll Show You What Grim is!

And every moment is a new and shocking
Valuation of all we have been

T. S. Eliot
Four Quartets (1943)

Lights come up.

[Among other things in this scene, Consciousness is struck and amused watching Hartman actually fall out of his chair and to his knees, calling out and begging there on the stage, as he dramatizes what painful emotions are like further and further back in a lifetime. The anguish in Hartman's voice when he utters the final "PLEEEEEEASE!!!!" is startling. It fills the whole theater. Consciousness is amazed that Hartman had it in him.]

And there you have it—seven facts about the present moment and seven feelings to cultivate, based on those facts, to find serenity. Seven roads to take into the present moment, and seven rules for a smooth ride.

Now we want this little rainbow of ingredients, hanging tenuously way up in the air of our minds, to blend together and, along with any other helpful ideas about change, become part of our awareness. We want them inside our cocoons with us, to weave in their truth, so we can turn them into living, working parts of ourselves, like caterpillars do when they make their wings.

To do this may take some studying. It's one thing to *see* a potentially life-changing rainbow of ideas and be all excited about the possibilities. It's another thing to make it such an integral part of ourselves that it actually helps us to get off the ground inside our minds and fly. But before we deal any further with cocoons, wings, or breakthrough points, there's a particular reaction these seven facts can lead to which has to be taken care of first. Okay, here they are again:

1. The present moment is here right now.
2. We have to give up needing to be loved in the ways we weren't loved enough as kids. Bye-bye old, lightless neutron stars—our amygdalae—we've been wishing upon, full of all of our childhood hope and disappointment! Bye-bye past!
3. We're completely alone inside our minds right now.
4. We're entirely responsible for the condition our awareness is in right now.
5. We never know very much about anything, especially right now.
6. We're insignificant and inessential in the whole scheme of things.
7. And we have to let the present moment go, too. Bye-bye everything.

And *this* is what leads to serenity, you ask? Sounds a little grim? You think so? Well, I'd like to show you what I think grim really is. I'd like to demonstrate for you how much of the time we're actually living by almost the opposite of these rules and, as a consequence, falling far away from Now into the troubled, never-enough world of our limbic system.

Okay, let's experience the seven facts and rules for being in the present moment as we fall back, in slow motion, further and further into the grip of our limbic mind. Let's see what it looks like at different points along the way. It'll be nothing new. We do this all the time on our own, though with much less warning and without the educational purpose we have together now. Let's start at a familiar place that's some distance from the present moment, but not too far back. Here we go (Each number refers to the corresponding fact about being in the present moment):

1. The present moment wouldn't be anything we took much notice of. We wouldn't think much about it. Most of the time, we probably wouldn't notice that we were in it, or that it's really here. We'd just be going about our business, with the universe reaching out in every direction all around us.

2. Ever so subtly, and without our knowing it, we'd be needing to be loved in ways we weren't loved enough in our childhoods. We'd be expressing this unconsciously in the ways we think, the goals we have, and the ways we try to be recognized, approved of, or admired, for what we do. And we'd be expressing it in the general fantasy we have about the way things should go wherever we happen to be: at work, at home, in supermarkets, in traffic, etc. And through any painful emotions that may flare up would be whispering our yearning for the love we never had enough of, without our knowing it.

3. We probably wouldn't be thinking much about how alone we are inside our minds right now. The thought we're actually completely alone inside would be alien. It wouldn't compute. "Of course I'm not alone," you would say. "There are people with me, and pets, and my computer, and so many things that are so alive right there with me," you would say. "What do you mean, I'm alone? That's silly," you would say.

4. We wouldn't really be taking full responsibility for the way we're feeling inside our minds right now. We probably wouldn't be thinking that our feelings about life only come from the inside of our minds. We'd be pretty sure that there are other forces—people, institutions, and nature—that may be responsible for making us feel the way we do.

5. We'd be thinking about what we know for sure about the world and what's going on out there right now. The thought wouldn't occur to us that we know almost nothing about anything all the time. We'd be swinging back and forth between being a little doubtful about things to being pretty convinced about what's going on. Back and forth …

6. We may be thinking with or without being much aware of it, that we don't get enough attention. We'd be wishing our point of view was more significant, believing that *we* were more significant and special than people ever knew, and that we ought to be more appreciated and respected than we are.

There's this vision we might have, a quiet subtle one, deep down, of how underappreciated we generally are—by our wife, husband, family, friends, our boss, landlord, our motor vehicle bureau, our credit card company, our lawyer, etc.

7. And we wouldn't be letting some things go as fast as they must go— thoughts, feelings, attitudes, vacations, people, things that break, the present moment, whatever …

*   *   *

Okay, now let's go even further away from Now and to a point still further back in time on the way to that oldest most painful feeling in each of our minds. And watch the negative feeling begin to flare a little more:

1. We'd be oblivious to the idea that there's a real present moment going on that's very mysterious. We wouldn't care about it at all. We'd have other things to do.

2. We'd be needing to be liked and loved a lot. We might be a little worried about upsetting people, wanting that great feeling of approval—wanting to be loved the way we weren't liked and loved enough as a kid, though we wouldn't think of it this way. Or we might just have an edge and want there to be a little more justice.

3. We'd be uneasy and restless being alone. We'd be hunting for amusement, needing pleasure and comfort.

4. We'd be refusing to take complete responsibility for our actions and for our feeling about life. We'd be convinced that in many instances someone or something else is what's making us feel and act the way we feel and act.

5. We'd be feeling a little insecure and want to know for sure what's really going on out there. Sometimes with people we'd be pretty sure we know exactly how they're thinking and feeling and why, and we'd be wishing they would think and feel a different way. We wouldn't be doing much real wondering about things and accepting that there are loads and loads of mystery out there.

6. We'd be thinking deep down that we really are very special in many ways and we really ought to be treated better. But we're not.

7. And we wouldn't want to let go of things that we don't want to let go of—attitudes, yearnings, grievances, among all kinds of other things.

*   *   *

Okay, now further back, and I will let the old feeling inside that's flaring up and pulling on us speak for itself about how it feels about the world:

"Please, I don't want you to tell me it's Now. What is that? I'm not feeling safe here. Love me! I just want you to love me. And don't leave me, please. I need you to be there. And I need you to take care of me, too, please. Take really good care of me! You should know how to. And please, I need to know for sure right now. I don't want to have to wonder about it! Please. And please, I need you to think I'm special! I really do. Please do. And please, I can't let go! I can't."

*   *   *

Okay, now even further back and, again, with the old feeling inside speaking:

"Pleease, I don't want to hear about Now!! **Pleease** don't tell me it's Now!! Just pleease, pleease love me!! And pleease *don't* leave me alone. I can't be alone now!! **Pleease,** don't stop taking care of me!! Pleease!! And pleease don't tell me I'm wrong about anything, ever**!!** Pleease!! And **Pleease** I need to know I'm very special to you. **Pleease** tell me you feel this way about me, and that way about me, and this way about me, and that way about me, and this way and that way and this way and that way!! **Pleeease!!** And **Pleeease**, don't tell me I have to let go!! **Pleeease!!** Don't ever do that!!"

*   *   *

Okay, even further back into the old pain:

"**Pleeeease,** I can't stand that it's Now!!! It's dangerous!!! Whatever you do, don't tell me it's Now!!! I don't want to know!!! **Pleeeease** love me!!!

Pleeeease!!! And **Pleeeease** don't ever leave me, **ever!!! Pleeeease!!! Pleeeease** take care of me forever and ever!!! And **Pleeeease** don't ever tell me I'm wrong, **damn it!!!** And **Pleeeease** tell me all the time I'm extremely special and important!!! I need to hear it**!!! All** the time**!!!** And **Pleeeease** I'm never gonna let go!!! … **Pleeeease!!!"**

*   *   *

Okay, now let's go all the way back and listen to the feeling. Here it is:

"PLEEEEE EASE!!!!"

Now this is real trouble. Does this sound like anyone you've known? This is where we could each go, and how bad it could get, when we don't accept what's true about being in this moment. It's dangerous to become frozen in an old painful moment like this one that's in another part of our brain but isn't actually happening anymore. And this is what I call grim.

Lights down.

Scene 38

Trick Question: Which One Will Help You the Most to Hold on to that Bucking Bronco We Call Our Limbic System— Its Magical Thinking or Your Effort?

Happy the man who early learns the wide chasm
that lies between his wishes and his powers.

Johann Wolfgang von Goethe
The Book of Positive Quotations (1993)

Lights come up.

[Among other things in this scene, Consciousness thinks about Hartman and his sense of humor. This time, Hartman yells "PLEEEEEESE!!!!" from his chair.]

Let's take a closer look at this oldest painful emotion that flares up through us from our limbic system when it's in a state of alarm, pulling us into its grip and taking us way back in time, far away from Now. Here it is again:

"PLEEEEE EASE!!!!"

What I want to point out is that there's no trace of serenity in it. There's a lot of pain—a strong, frustrated yearning for some kind of magic to happen, and quickly, because of how dangerous reality feels even when there's no real danger. Listen carefully to the need for magic:

"PLEEEEE EASE!!!!"

Do you hear it? It's begging for magic, screaming for it. And you can tell by its painful sound how very much it's demanding something else to be happening besides what's happening right now, demanding to be living so very far away from Now. And notice how it's rejecting the seven rules for being in the present moment:

1. There's almost no tolerance for the enigmatic presence of Now. There's very little *courage* being displayed here to deal with Now.

2. There's an overpowering need for love of some kind, but no appreciation for whatever *new kinds of love* there might be.

3. The feeling of being alone seems quite unbearable. There's not much of a sense of *inner security* or *self-reliance*.

4. There seems to be no interest in taking much responsibility for anything. There's very little self-confidence, very little sense of *competence*.

5. There's clearly a terrible need to know something for sure, and not much of a sense of *wonderment*.

6. There's a desperate need to be considered very special and significant, and not a trace of *humility*. A lot of humiliation, but no humility.

7. And there seems to be an agonizing inability to let go, and not a bit of real *sorrow*.

Let's listen again:

"PLEEEEE EASE!!!!"

This is the feeling we fall under the spell of when we're at our worst, when we're not making any of the necessary efforts to be in *this* moment. This awful feeling needs a completely different kind of moment from the only one there is, and it gets us to believe this, too.

Fierce anger could flare out of this old feeling and then right through us. And when it flares, we'll demand a new boss, and immediately. And a different neighbor. And different leaders in the world. And we'll need our wife to be different from the way she is right now. And we'll need our husband to be different from the way he is right now. And the feeling could flare into terrible worry, desperation or resentment. We'll need our skin problems, sinus problems, back problems, and hemorrhoids to be gone, just like that! We'll need for our enemies to have them, or worse. We'll need cancer to never have been there, and to not be hanging over our heads. We'll need our bank accounts filled even more. We'll need the sun to be shining where the rain clouds are. And maybe for summer to be where winter is. In other words, when we're under the influence of this old feeling, we might actually need the entire Earth to be moved further along, or back, in its orbit around the Sun, immediately, so we can have the season we want instead of the one we're in.

Well, I'm sorry, but we just have to respect the mass and position of a heavenly body like the Earth. As well as all the rest of them in the universe—the only universe that happens to be available at the moment. And if you ask me, the heavenly bodies we ought to be turning our attention to and changing our attitudes about are the limbic ones inside our own brain that are pulling the life out us.

Lights down.

Scene 39

HopeHopeHopeHopeHopeHopeHope

She was within a few steps of it, and Oz was holding out his hands to help her into the basket, when, crack! went the ropes, and the balloon rose into the air without her.
'Come back!' she screamed. 'I want to go, too!' ...
Dorothy wept bitterly at the passing of her hope to get home to Kansas again.

L. Frank Baum
The Wonderful Wizard of Oz (1900)

Lights come up.

[Among other things in this scene, Consciousness is a little dismayed by how intensely alive Hartman seems to become when he's busy stripping away practically everything there is that a person can rely on.]

Don't lose all hope, Dorothy! Only most of it! And wake up! That's how you get back to Kansas. *Now* is waiting for you.

One of the hardest things about changing is accepting that a kind of hope is going to pass away. Giving up the hope you have and have had is at the very heart of the kind of change that deepens and steadies someone. Old hope like this has to be given up for new hope to be embraced.

All of our lives, we've lived with and known a certain kind of hope. At the core of every painful emotion there is old hope. Every moment of yearning and disappointment stored in our brain is permeated with it, all the wild and quiet hopes of childhood: the hope that all will go well, that the world will be safe for us and that we will be loved, and that the love will be exactly as we dreamed—so strong and so right. And when it comes, it will say, "You are so very lovable. I love you more than you can know. You're more precious than my words can say. I'm so happy you're alive. I'll love you forever. And I'll always be there for you. Always."

This is the hope we'll have to be able to let go of and not be dependent upon any more if all goes well. This is the anguished hope in our painful emotions that flares up in our minds over and over and misguides us. What's acceptable to it has to be so perfect that it's never fulfilled for long, or at all.

This hope radiating from all of our old disappointed yearnings is at the very heart of our emotional problems in life, and our whole species' problem on the worldwide scale. And it's hard to pull our awareness away from it because it's the only hope we've ever known. It's hard to even imagine being without it, because we never have been. That's why the seven facts about being in the moment can sound so grim. It's because of the sharp contrast between the strange calm in these facts and the aching hope for fantastic magic emanating from the negative feelings that flare up through our brains from our limbic system. This hope holds our oldest and deepest optimism. It may be what has kept us going. Without it, we might fear plunging into utter despair.

But there's a tremendous difference between giving up this old hope for magic to happen and being in despair. There's a state of mind for us in between our old hope and despair which is very neutral, calm, and hopeful in a whole new, flexible way.

Each of the seven facts about the present moment involves a loss. Each one is a way to help let some of this hope go and move to that more serene, simpler place:

1. Recognizing and accepting that there's a present moment which is deeply mysterious by its very nature implies giving up, letting go of, the hope for whatever reality you're needing or demanding to be there instead.
2. Giving up needing to be loved the way you weren't loved enough as a child means letting go of the hope for this magical, perfect love.
3. Believing that you're alone inside means letting go of the hope for an unrealistic and very often unavailable kind of closeness.

4. Accepting full responsibility for yourself means letting go of the hope of being taken care of right now exactly the way you've yearned to be.

5. Admitting how little you can know in this moment means letting go of the hope for absolute certainty, which even the physicists, the most precise of scientists, believe is out of the question.

6. Acknowledging your true insignificance in the scheme of things means letting go of the hope for being as special right now to the outside world as you always needed so much to be.

7. And realizing that even the present moment passes away means letting go of the hope that you can hold on to what there's no way to hold on to, namely anything and everything.

Being in the moment is very much about loss, letting it all go. I'm not talking here about the kind of loss you feel when someone dies, but the experience of loss you induce in yourself by realizing you don't have and never have had what you've always believed you had and could always have. It's a very special kind of loss. When things change for the better, there's so much you lose, so much you give away. And there will be sorrow about this, not sadness, fear, defeat, or despair; just some sorrow, a bridge to acceptance.

Then a different kind of hope will grow; one that has everything to do with Now. It'll be a hope that changes as Now changes. It won't ever stay the same, like the old hope for that one perfect thing, because Now never stays the same. Every moment needs a different kind of hope, because every moment has a brand new universe in it.

Lights down.

S c e n e 4 0

Going from Here to **Here**.
(Or, When Fabulous Progress Doesn't Feel Like Any Progress at All. Ah, Those Growing Pains Again.)

We're here
Because
We're here.

Sung to the tune of 'Auld Lang Syne',
in John Brophy and Eric Partridge
Songs and Slang of the British Soldier
1914–1918 (1930)

Lights come up.

[*Among other things in this scene, Consciousness thinks how very strange a job Hartman has trying to set off all of these quiet little explosions in people's minds, and why he keeps doing it without ever being able to know for sure if it ever gets done.*]

All kidding aside, some people think I just sit on my ass all day. But appearances are deceptive. It's strenuous work facilitating these breakthroughs. It may look like I'm just sitting around here in my chair having pleasant conversations. I'm actually busy flying in and out of the stormy skies in people's minds, trying to get them ready for a big change, a big metamorphosis.

The activity that goes on in the course of an emotional breakthrough—from the first moment of my encounter with someone to the end of our work—is an awesome, almost miraculous thing to be part of. Strenuous effort that can generate its own kind of pain is involved for both of us. But it's very different from the emotional pain that brings anyone into my office. This effort in our work steps up the pain. I help amplify it in a controlled way by guiding your awareness to its source inside your brain, taking you closer to it to appreciate its force and the thinking it's made of.

The ultimate goal is for you to go all the way and try to free yourself from the

"PLEEEEE EASE!!!!"

inside your brain that can flare up and consume you, making you believe there's danger where there isn't. The whole point of appreciating the intensity of the pull of emotional pain is to break its spell, to steal its thunder. You work to take the wind out of its sails and use it to build new strength and direction into your awareness. You overpower its grip whenever it might threaten to flare through you, so it doesn't interfere as much with your experience of life in *this* very moment, no matter what may be going on.

You put yourself through something strange when you're undertaking this thing called a breakthrough. It may feel strange each time you have to do it for yourself, even after you've done it once. You have to concentrate hard on those seven facts about Now, or ideas like them, and know all about the essence of those old feelings beginning to flare up inside which are busy rejecting the present moment and yearning for one that has been magically transformed. And as you work toward a breakthrough, it may not feel like you're making any progress. It may just feel like confusion, helplessness, bewilderment, and frustration. It may feel like wild winds are blowing around inside, and blowing you around with them. The very best progress may not feel like any progress at all. That's why I'm sitting here, or someone like me. I'm the personal trainer putting you through the circuit, stressing the hell out of you, to strengthen you.

And there will be resistance in you. I know. You'll think you don't know what you're doing. It may feel humiliating having to rely on me. You're vulnerable in the throes of your pain. And you'll doubt my ability along the way. In your doubt and frustration, you're telling me that you're following everything I've been talking about, but it's not enough because no big change is happening and you're not feeling any better. You're telling me, "There's something missing from the method, Dr. Psychologist. You think you have it all together with this limbic system business and this talk about the present moment. Yes, Doctor, it all sounds very cool and looks nice on paper. But it's missing something, because it's not working!"

What's missing and what's decisive has to do with the power with which you learn to see, and understand, and realize, and believe. There's seeing,

and there's **seeing**. There's understanding,

and   there's   **under-standing**. There's realizing

something about your life, and **realiz-**

ing something about your life. When you

realize something about your life consistently enough, it has a chance to go on and become a

belief that can give off such strong energy from your awareness that it may even change the way your DNA works. And you will live better for it.

Realizations don't have a chance of becoming new beliefs the way

realizations do. Even **realizations** are better than realizations. A lot of people think they're

having **realizations** or **realizations**

or **realizations** when they're only having **realizations**, or just realizations, or maybe even realizations.

The seven facts about Now that help free us from our old pain and take us into the serenity in this moment aren't just gimmicks or sleights of hand we use on ourselves to achieve a certain artificially calm state of mind. There are no tricks. The psychological distance we travel from the past into

Now is real. These seven facts describe a destination. And they imply the routes we take, what we give up along the way, and the rules of the road we have to follow to get there, wherever in the past we happen to have fallen.

And we each have to doubt them until we have no doubts about them anymore. Then they become very powerful, and we accept them as some of the simplest truths we could hope to live by.

There's a vague sense we each have that we're on some kind of odyssey as we go through life. How we get from

seeing   to   **seeing**   and   from

understanding   to   **under-standing**,   from

realizing   to   **realizing**,

from   acceptance   to   **accep-**

tance, and from believing to **believing**, is what

inner transformation, and the journey into the present moment, and therapy, are all about. The distance between these, with everything that's lost and gained on the way, is what we humans are trying to travel in our lives. This distance is our odyssey.

The big ones are the ones with the real wing power. And they don't take us to paradise or to a more perfect moment. The big ones, when they become a part of us, are the ones that help us travel out of the darker past inside our brain and into *this* moment, where the real light of day is, no matter what chaos is there.

And I go after the big ones when I do therapy. This is how I believe we grow the strength to go from here to **here**. This is the plan. And I can't do this by just sitting on my ass.

Lights down.

Scene 41

The Butterfly Kit. How Many Butterflies Break Through Their Cocoons Each Day? So When is it Your Turn?

Our remedies oft in ourselves do lie
Which we ascribe to heaven.

William Shakespeare
All's Well that Ends Well (1623)

Lights come up.

[Among other things in this scene, Consciousness thinks about Hartman walking around in a garden and wonders when he'll finally decide to retire and never do therapy again.]

There's a butterfly kit you can buy that promises to make you butterflies. Included in the kit is a coupon you mail away for five cosmopolite (world citizen) butterfly caterpillars. There's a cube you unfold and put together that's about the size of a globe of the world, with large, round cellophane windows on all sides for you to watch your butterflies emerge from their chrysalises. The caterpillars are sent to you when the weather is right. When they arrive, they will be five unassuming little animals in a round plastic container voraciously eating what looks like dirt.

In a few days, the caterpillars swell with their food and fatten up. Then at a certain moment, without any fanfare, each one climbs up to the lid of the container, attaches itself, and hardens into a chrysalis. The lid has a circular layer of adhesive wax paper you peel off and paste on the wall inside the cardboard door of the windowed cube you put together. The chrysalises will hang down a little from the inside wall.

About ten days later, over the course of several hours, the butterflies will imperceptibly begin tearing through their chrysalises. As you watch them do this, for quite a while it looks like nothing is happening. It looks like they're not making any progress at all, as though they're at a complete standstill. But they're actually making wonderful progress as they strain to break through. And the effort they make to do this is crucial for their survival. The strain of squeezing themselves out is what makes their wing muscles grow strong enough to be able to fly, find food and mate. If you try in any way to help the butterflies emerge from their chrysalises, their wings won't grow strong enough, and they'll starve. You'll hurt them terribly if you try to help them out. They need to struggle out by themselves, alone, to concentrate on those wing muscles, and build enough strength in them to fly and live and mate in the present moments of their short lives.

And then, when they're out and their wings are all dried and pumped up, you take them outside with your feeling for them, you open the door of their cube, let them go, and the vivid butterflies are ... **gone** *and traveling the wide world ...*

Lights down.

Scene 42

The Breakthrough Point. Where is It?
Now Where is that Thing? I Know It's
Around Here Somewhere. Could Someone

Please Aim the Light
Over Here?

Dorothy to Glinda, after the Wizard took off in his balloon:
"Oh, will you help me? Can you help me?"

from the movie
The Wizard of Oz (1939)

Clarence! Clarence! Help me, Clarence. Get me back. Get me
back. I don't care what happens to me. Only get me back ... Help
me, Clarence, please. Please! I want to live again.

from the movie
It's a Wonderful Life (1946)

Lights come up.

[Among other things in this scene, Consciousness thinks about Hartman in his
own therapy dealing with those struggles he had with work and love, what he
was once like and what it must have been like being his therapist.]

Okay, so where exactly does a breakthrough actually begin? Does it begin
when you're going through a bad bout of emotional pain? Or does it begin
when you seek help for the pain? Or does a breakthrough begin some time

even before you experience your pain and leads to your pain? Does a breakthrough begin somewhere back in your childhood without you knowing it? Does it begin at birth? Before birth? Was the beginning of the breakthrough you'll have later in life gleaming in your parents' minds way before they had you? Or was the breakthrough already stirring in the stardust which exploded from a star long ago and ultimately became you?

Everyone who wants to change ought to be wondering about this and asking these questions, or questions like them, in order to get at some sense of the truth about it.

And what about the breakthrough *point* of a breakthrough. Where is that? For a caterpillar, is it when it emerges from its chrysalis as a butterfly? Or is it when it goes into its chrysalis? Or is it when, inside its chrysalis, it creates wings where there were none before?

And for us humans who are in some sort of treatment, is the breakthrough point at the end of the breakthrough, at the climax, when it's just about over? Or is the breakthrough point actually at the very beginning, where it all starts? Or is it before the beginning? Or is there one kind of breakthrough point at the beginning of the process that sets it off, and one kind at the end, where it culminates? And might there be lots of smaller breakthrough points along the way? Wouldn't a real, life-changing emotional breakthrough be a regular racket of breakthrough points, from the first one to the last? I mean, there is a beginning and an end to things, isn't there?

And what about the end? Does the breakthrough point at the end come at some kind of crescendo of your efforts, and then a wave of serenity spreads through you? Or does a capacity for serenity grow in fits and starts as your strength grows, reaching some sort of final growth at the end and becoming a reliable state of mind in your life? And do you hear a loud sound when you're at the final breakthrough point? Do you writhe in a fit of agony? Do you scream for joy and hop around? Or are you just quiet?

I know we entertain the possibility of a breakthrough for a long time before we actually undertake to have one. We do a lot of entertaining before we decide in earnest to have a breakthrough. For a long time, we hope it won't take too long or be too much of a strain. I know this, too. We do lots of hoping before we get serious about having one.

That Certain "Something" and the "Nothing" it Comes From

If you've gotten this far, you've followed most of what I've said. But this doesn't mean a breakthrough is really underway yet. Something has to happen at the very beginning of a breakthrough for it to begin. A certain "something" has to coalesce in you that sets the whole thing into motion and drives it along. I believe this is the most decisive thing about a breakthrough. This, you could say, is the most decisive breakthrough point at the beginning of the breakthrough. I've gotten good at spotting it when it's there. And when I do spot it, I know the breakthrough is well on its way. But getting it into place in a person is a major, crucial accomplishment. It's a little mysterious and elusive. It may be well into the therapy process before it's there. Without it, there's no hope of a breakthrough ever happening. With it, it's guaranteed. Then it becomes just a matter of steady work and time.

This "something" has been referred to by my colleagues as the motivation for change. It has strong elements of commitment and determination and courage and maybe a kind of faith as well. It's a highly potent blend. And I find I must aim and focus carefully to kindle it.

All emotional breakthroughs come from this "something." It's not exactly a part of what's so visible during a breakthrough. It comes before the whole thing, stays in the heart of it, and fills it with life and direction. And yet, in a way, this "something" sort of is the breakthrough. It's the driving force, the very soul of it.

My most strenuous work with a person largely comes to an end when I know this "something" is finally there. When we firmly establish the motivation, the commitment, and the determination to change—when we discover the steel in his or her will—a crucial beginning phase of the work ends, like when the liftoff of a space mission has been successful and the spacecraft is well on its way from the force of the blastoff. Still, the trajectory of the mission also has to be checked carefully along the way and the ship has to be steered well to get to its destination.

This "something" in our minds is at the growing edge for us humans on our journey. These moments with you have been my attempt to help set it off. The way I've spoken and all I've said about how our painful emotions flare from a part of our brain radiating with it's old fear of death, and about the fight and flight designed into these very emotions, and what you do to free yourself—all of this has been my way to help ignite this "something." I've been trying to prepare the conditions for a huge spark to light up in your mind.

But seeing what I've told you is so necessary, too. There's all I've told you, and there's you seeing all I've told you. They're two different things. And they're both so important. Right there is where you and I make contact. Right there between what I say and what you see, we touch (long pause).

And what's still more mysterious about this "something" has to do only with you—not me: it's you alone who lights the spark deep within the seeing you do so silently inside the cocoon of your mind. It's yours to make and to have. I can do my best to help coax it into being. I can try with all my heart to help bring it to life. But I can't create it; only you can. And I have a feeling this ability to spark that "something" is just what people are looking for out there in the world. In self-help books, weekend retreats, love affairs, and all sorts of other places. And it may be just what our civilization needs to set off a needed transformation of our whole species.

This "something" at the beginning of a breakthrough is surely a very sacred thing. Once the conditions are right for it, it seems to come right out of nowhere, out of nothing, and new awareness comes surging out along with it.

Similarly, before the entire universe itself was compressed into a size smaller that the point of a needle, there was this "nothing" it emerged from. Just like an emotional breakthrough. And they're probably somehow related to one another. Whether you're a caterpillar or a Consciousness or a cosmos, something new comes out of a kind of "nothing" and this huge change happens and the whole paradigm shifts. This is the sort of influence I strive to have on you. I try to touch you where there's not enough, where sometimes it feels like there's nothing at all. And I try to convince you with everything I have, with all of my faith, that a new way of being is possible, that a whole new universe can come to life out of nothing, and keep becoming Now.

So was it when Dorothy clicked the ruby slippers together that she was on her way home? Or was it when her foot stepped onto those first yellow bricks on the way to Oz? Or was she on her way home when she landed in Munchkinland? Or maybe she was on her way home before she began to dream, when she was knocked out by the flying window frame during the tornado in Kansas. Or maybe the beginning of her journey home began even before that, in her unhappiness, when she was with Professor Marvel and he was gazing into his crystal ball, pretending to see into her life. Maybe it was there, when she let him touch her pain, her emptiness, and that "something" came to life and made it possible for her to dream about home and go all the way...

Lights down.

Scene 43

It's The Most Radical Pause a Human Can
Make. It's The Most Radical Human Pause
of All in the Whole Shooting Match of Life,
in the Whole Barrel of Pickles, the Whole Box
of Crayons … it's Serenity!
And it Gets Hammered Together Out of
Acceptance that You're Inside Your Mind
Right Now Living Your Life,
and Out of Courage, and Love,
and Self-reliance, and Responsibility, and
Wonder, and Humility, and Loss, and
Sorrow, and Forgiveness, and Realistic Hope,
and Gratitude, and a Bunch of Other Things, Too.

There was never any more inception than there is now
… And will never be any more perfection than there is now.

Walt Whitman
Song of Myself (1881)

Everything has its wonders, even darkness and silence.

Helen Keller
The Story of My Life (1903)

The only courage that matters is the kind that gets you from one moment to the next.

Mignon McLaughlin
The Second Neurotic's Notebook (1966)

Then dawns the Invisible; the Unseen its truth reveals;
My outward sense is gone, my inward essence feels:
Its wings are almost free—its home, its harbor found,
Measuring the gulf, it stoops, and dares the final bound.

Emily Brontë
The Prisoner (A Fragment) (1846)

This is the beginning, the spark shot free
That gnaws and widens into living flame

Dante Alighieri
The Divine Comedy (ca. 1307)

You must habit yourself to the dazzle of the light and of every moment of your life.

Walt Whitman
Song of Myself (1881)

I am prepared to press on to the end along a road in which each step makes me more certain, toward horizons that are ever more shrouded in mist.

Pierre Teilhard de Chardin
How I Believe (1969)

And I, who neared the goal of all my nature,
felt my soul, at the climax of its yearning,
suddenly, as it ought, grow calm with rapture.

Dante Alighieri
The Divine Comedy (ca. 1307)

And I say to any man or woman, Let your soul stand cool
and composed before a million universes.

> Walt Whitman
> *Song of Myself* (1881)

The mere sense of living is joy enough.

> Emily Dickinson
> *Selected Poems & Letters*
> *of Emily Dickinson* (1959)

The surest sign of the higher life is serenity
… progress results in freedom from inner turmoil.

> Epictetus
> *Encheiridion: The Manual for*
> *Living* (ca. A.D. 125)

Remember, this day will not dawn again.

> Dante Alighieri
> *The Divine Comedy* (ca. 1307)

… a lifetime burning in every moment …
… and the time of death is every moment …

> T. S. Eliot
> *Four Quartets* (1943)

Thank you for a lovely time

> Janet Churchill Greene
> (1917–1997)
> Inscription on her gravestone
> Mountain View Cemetery
> West Dover, Vermont

Lights come up.

[*Among many other things in this scene, Consciousness watches the afternoon sunlight driving deeply into the office, making everything glow, and notices how vulnerable Hartman seems sometimes even when he's speaking in his calm reassuring tone.*]

When that "something" is finally there inside of you, it speaks with conviction, saying: "You have to hold back that dark feeling mounting in you right now and change how you are about to react. And you will." And as it speaks in its strong, quiet way, you'll be more comfortable engaging in this work all the way through your metamorphosis into a you with the knowhow, skill and determination to move yourself more deliberately and conscientiously out of the disabling grip of your painful emotion and into the wide-open present moment. You'll be better at letting go of what doesn't really matter now and embracing what simply does.

And along the way, you'll notice the time it takes to influence your mind as you work with your pain and all of the moments and distances that are inside. It won't be like firing a shot with a strong sound and an immediate impact. Rather, it'll be like moving toward something, like the waves set into motion in the wake of a large ship passing by, far out at sea. The waves heave into life at the passing of the ship and start rolling along, taking time to reach you at the shore. There's a delay between when you begin to realize you've fallen back into the grip of your past, engulfed by a painful feeling, and when you prompt yourself to set about breaking free of it. And there's a delay between when you try to break free from the feeling and when you do. It takes time for all of the waves of realization to move through your system. You'll pause and notice these delays. And then, as you're standing there at the shore, the waves begin to churn a little differently and crash with a little more energy, and you know they came from that large ship that sailed by way out at sea. You saw when those very waves were set into motion out there and wondered when they would arrive, and you feel how long they took to reach you. Maybe these delays are there in us because we're made of the sea. The neurons at the bottom and at the edges of our minds are still made of the sea. Our minds are made of time and our neurons are made of the sea. So everything takes time. And no one will know these delays as well as you. These are your own private delays to encounter and respect, always.

So when emotional pain flares again from deep within your brain, as it surely will, you'll know to go to the beginning of yourself where that "something" is that sets you into motion, where you discover again the steel in your will to dispel the dark, unhelpful old thinking that generates your pain. That spark you can find at the beginning of yourself in each new moment is your source of power to contend with all things. And it's always there for you.

Actually, the huge spark that began the universe is always there with us in every moment. It's such an idea to behold that if we could see far enough away right now we would see the first moments, the beginning of everything, where all of the energy is that set everything into motion. We're all still bathing in a sea of photons remaining from those first moments. The beginning is all around us. And this beginning out there is so different from the past collected inside our minds from childhood, so different from our limbic mind where all of our darkness is, where there's a pained yearning for a very different universe. This beginning has all of the actual energy and force that everything real has come from. And it's always with us, waiting for us to acknowledge and be inspired by.

What you do as a human who deals with moments is to train yourself to be there at the onset of each new moment, each instant of your life. You find the energy you need there at the beginning. Each moment is a fractal of all time, and each moment has a powerful beginning to it, just like the very first one. And when you find yourself in pain, you go back to that something in you, that potent blend of interest, commitment, determination, faith, and whatever else is there at the beginning of you right now that sets you into motion toward life. And you manage once again to undertake the journey no one sees you take to get all the way back to Now, to contend with the strange, challenging collection of conditions awaiting you there.

And that's the kind of process psychotherapy is, too. You go on a journey, learning anew to understand the problem. You gather insights about the way to solve it and experience a few promising effects. Maybe you become very enthusiastic about the possibility of making the process of breaking through a part of yourself. And then you're back at the beginning again, having to consider giving yourself over wholeheartedly to the goal of doing it.

Here's a tricky situation to consider. When a star goes out and it's far enough away, deep enough in the past, you still see its light for a long time, because the light hitting your eye left that star and travelled away when it was still lit. And so you believe, as you watch the star's light, that it's coming from a star that's still alive. And you might even wish upon it, even though it might have gone out long ago. But what's going on in the present moment for that star up there is impossible for you to know about because you're too far away from it.

But the star that has gone out inside your own mind is different. This situation isn't so tricky. It may be the past, the very distant past, but it's with you now, right there inside your mind. You can know that old star inside—your limbic system—has gone out and isn't to be looked up to anymore because you're in the present moment now which is here to help you determine what possibilities and limitations exist for you now, what doesn't exist anymore, and what you can no longer be, have, or wish for.

So you will surely fall away once again, and then again, into the past inside. And you'll struggle back there with its pull. But you can find that "something" at the beginning of yourself and it will prompt you to give up wishing upon that old star—dreaming of perfection that can never be—and start working, pausing, in the discomfort of your pain, to travel back to the fullness of Now.

And when that "something" has wakened in you, you'll also be more comfortable with how much loss there is, with how much you have to learn to lose as you become free of your feelings of pain. Remember, you're trying to *part ways* with your pain—your anxiety, anger, fear. All of it. Not so that you can be free of it completely by obliterating it once and for all, forevermore. That can never happen, because the past will always be there inside with you and could flare up again whenever there's an obstacle. It could pull you back all of a sudden, when you're not looking. And besides, you don't want to forget your past and your old feelings. No, you're just trying, with your sights on Now, to part ways with your painful emotions by pulling free of them, declaring a boundary, letting go of their disenchantment. You're leaving them behind, just for now.

There's real loss here: deep, personal loss. You keep saying good-bye all through your life to all of the old yearning in you for *magic* love as you travel back into Now. It won't be an ordinary or simple good-bye. It will grow to feel like a complex good-bye that resonates in a strange, quiet sort of way and leaves you in a stillness. All good-byes might begin to feel like this for you. And even hellos. And what's between the hellos and the good-byes might, too.

And there'll be those moments, maybe extended moments—maybe summertimes or winters—when all of your good-byes will blend together with your acceptance and your courage and become the calmest, steadiest response to what's going on right now, whatever that may be, with all of its millions and millions of limitations and possibilities.

You'll feel just simply in the heart of yourself. And grateful to be there. Grateful that there are molecules.

And you'll spend all of your best days traveling through your mind this way toward Now, where we all have to live and work, where all the full light is. Because this is what you do: you live and move around in time. And if all goes well, you make finding calm and steadiness an accomplished skill, not just an accident of circumstance or biochemistry.

And someday, when you're asked if you're fulfilled, or content, or happy, you'll say: "Yes, I am. Because of what I lose all day. I feel loss all day long. That's how I feel so calm and enjoy so much of everything that's here. I feel the loss of everything all day. And I keep trying to give everything up all the time, every moment." That's what you'll say.

And so as that "something" is about to ignite in you, you'll be right there in the stillness you've made—ready for the beginning …

Lights down.

Scene 44

And So Ladies and Gentlemen, We've Come to the End Of Our Show. As They Say in This Biz— That's All There is; There isn't Any More. You've Been a Wonderful Audience. And I Want You All to Know, and with My Heart and Soul, that _This_ is What I Think Will Stop Us Humans from Finding Our Serenity:

Lights remain down. The entire theater is in darkness.

[_For a moment, in the total darkness and the huge hush, Consciousness was able to think of_ **nothing**.]

The End

Lights come up.

DR. HARTMAN: "Our time is up."

HUMAN CONSCIOUSNESS: Looks at Hartman, stands up, goes slowly out of the office, through the waiting room, and Human Consciousness is ... **gone** and *traveling the wide world ...*

Curtain

About the Author

Fredric C. Hartman is a clinical psychologist in private practice since 1988. He works and makes his home on Long Island, New York. Visit him online at www.TheBreakthroughBook.net.